MW01156713

Published in the United States of America

ISBN: 1442114525

EAN-13: 9781442114524

Manufactured in the United States of America
First Edition Published 2009

Front Cover Photo: Temple of the Bees © 2009 Nirvan Hope
Back Photo and Jacket Design: Nirvan Hope
Author Photo: Roy Nettlebeck

THREE SEASONS OF BEES
AND
OTHER
NATURAL AND UNNATURAL
THINGS

A Pacific Northwest Journal

NIRVAN HOPE

DEDICATION

To the river and wild nature
To Roy
To the bees
And beekeepers of the future

ACKNOWLEDGMENTS

Without Roy Nettlebeck, this book would not have been possible. He taught me everything I know about beekeeping and accompanied me on many of the adventures in this book, patiently waiting while I jotted down notes and asked multiple questions. He took me on journeys of discovery to wild places in nature and instilled in me a respect and love of bees and their way of life. Thanks are due also to Ian Nettlebeck, who with his wacky teenage ways, was a welcome companion, making some of the hard work much easier.

I am indebted to the core members of the Olympic Point of View Writers Group, past and present. The group has been an unwavering source of support and encouragement over the years: Shirley Cooper, Dianna Timm Dryden, Allie Durrie, Nettie Harper, Valerie West, David Snider, Gary Seelig, and Melinda Seelig. Thank you. My life has been considerably enriched by those Friday afternoon writes! Special thanks to Nettie Harper for her wise editorial suggestions and to Tom Coroneos for his invaluable proof reading. Any errors and flaws still within the book are entirely mine after I made last minute tweaks and changes.

Too many friends to mention have, with love and encouragement, seen me through the long process of writing, editing and publication. In particular I'd like to thank Salena Levi, Madir Thackeray, Shanti Shivani, Anne Reilly, Richard Greene, and Hilary Leighton. Others I have failed to mention, you know who you are! Thanks especially go to Aaron and Rose Collings who took me in when things fell apart. I am also grateful to Nikki Smith, who, after plowing through an early draft, offered her suggestion for the title of the book, and to Monty Smith for providing a roof over my head while I wrote.

I don't know how I would have made it through so many hours at the computer and editing the manuscript without the background of an eclectic mixture of instrumental music. Many thanks are due to the musicians who inspired me and kept me company on this journey.

My deepest gratitude goes to the honeybees, the Tahuya River, and all the wild nature that befriended me during my years on the Tahuya and Olympic Peninsula.

☼

CONTENTS

Introduction

Part 1: Spring

Part Two: Summer

Part Three: Spring

INTRODUCTION

RETURNING TO the Pacific Northwest after a five-year hiatus in the high desert of New Mexico, needing to re-hydrate and tired of the search for an elusive sense of place, I settled with a beekeeper, Roy Nettlebeck, on his five acres by the Tahuya River. I had come home. I quickly put down roots, grew to love the bees, beekeeping and organic country life. My domestic instincts thrived, while my love of nature reveled in the fertile earth, the healing forests and sparkling rivers of the Pacific Northwest.

Slipping into the role of assistant beekeeper, I helped assemble hives, tend bees, catch swarms, set up bee yards and move bees in seasonal migrations to and from the Olympic Mountains. I harvested hive products, extracted and bottled honey, worked with wax and sold at farmers markets. Roy had kept bees for more than thirty years and answered my endless questions with infinite patience.

Whenever free from beekeeping and markets, I spent many happy hours exploring the forested acres around my home. Time stretched in blissful ways I had never imagined as I wandered by the Tahuya River or tended the big unruly garden in our forest clearing. Backwoods, rivers and lakes of North Mason County became my playground. I wrapped myself in a soulful relationship with nature deeper than at any previous time in my life.

In early 2002, I began recording daily revelations of the natural world with photographs. At the same time I kept a journal of my days in nature, of beekeeping and other things, and it is from those scrawled notes that I have mined and mixed the ingredients for this book. Much of it describes nature's progress through the seasons, in particular, her plants and flowers—for I am sure that that is what the bees would know.

The events of that spring, summer and fall were extraordinary. Beekeeping was always interesting, hard work, and sometimes scary. Natural adventures unfolded with the rescue of a baby eagle, bee swarms, bear sightings and the iconic drama of spawning salmon in our backyard. River wading, mushroom hunting and gardening offered gentler Northwest pleasures. But, as if to balance the slow, sweet tempo of pastoral bliss, and parallel to settling ever deeper into my love affair with the land, with Roy, and the business of bees and honey, outside influences arrived that summer to shake and shadow our lives and our small community in the Tahuya forest.

Often, while beekeeping or hiking, reminders of a not-so-happy world pricked at the edges of my awareness: the world of bee-yard vandals, clear cuts, trash, illegal brush pickers, and frightening found objects. But none of these compared to the threat that moved onto the neighboring property. For seven months we lived with an escalating undercurrent of unease, frustration and paranoia spawned by the shadowy presence of suspected identity thieves and meth labs.

Although Roy was my constant companion throughout this time, this book is not about our relationship, (that would fill a whole other book). Instead, the journey through three seasons described on these pages attempts to share the joy of my relationship to the natural world as a love song or a dance. Two other threads kept me well grounded: beekeeping, and a glimpse of a darker side of rural life in Western Washington at the beginning of the twenty-first century.

PART 1

SPRING

CHAPTER 1

NEW BEES

ANOTHER STORM rumbles in from the west, with five more days of rain in the forecast. Only the bravest or most foolhardy bees fly in this fickle April weather and there's almost no activity at hive entrances. On sunny days earlier this year, excited by warm weather, bees hauled loads of pollen from pussy willow, dandelion and salmonberry. Queens laid eggs, new brood hatched daily. Bee populations expanded like popcorn. But now rain confines bees inside their hives, and even though they know exactly where nearby blossoms offer sweet nectar, few bees venture out. If surprised by the chill of a sudden shower, a bee's temperature drops fast and her fragile life soon fades.

I wander up the driveway to check beehives in the orchard. Flashes of color and movement behind cascara bushes become the brilliant feather-tufted red crown of a pileated woodpecker ruffling through leaves. I edge closer. The bird knows I've seen him. Hiding behind an alder trunk, he pokes an inquisitive head around twice, strikes two hasty pecks, then dashes off through the woods to a tall fir where he hops up the trunk and out of sight to excavate a grubby dinner from oblong holes that tattoo the trees.

Several pairs of the flashy woodpeckers call the Tahuya peninsula home, each pair claiming approximately four-hundred-and-fifty acres. As people encroach on their territory and the forests change, will the birds cover a larger area? Or leave the area completely to look for other forests? Or will they, while no one pays attention, slowly become extinct? At least the possibility of bee extinction is gaining public attention.

At one orchard hive, a single wet bee, chilled from last night's sudden rain, fumbles and drags weak legs across the hive lid like an arthritic woman. I watch her feeble struggle, then move away to the next hive, but as soon as I leave, know that I could have helped her to the entrance board. Regretting my callousness, I hurry back to her rescue but she has disappeared. Did she make it safely back into the comfort of her honey-sweet home? I leave the hives, hoping she survived.

☼

The bees are a constant source of wonder, and in early spring, Roy and I anticipate coming months of beekeeping adventure like explorers before an extended expedition.

Tending a hundred and twenty hives, sometimes more, sometimes less, in eight or nine locations, moving hives several times a year, we encourage the bees to gather pollen and nectar from the widest possible menu choice of wildflowers. We over-winter the bees in lowlands around the Hood Canal, chauffeur them to Olympic foothills in early summer, then drive them high into the Olympic Mountains for a late summer and fall harvest.

Choosing not to contract our hives for pollination of corporate monoculture farming, we only harvest wildflower honey from environments with minimum pollution, away from pesticides and herbicides. We also maintain a safe distance from other beekeepers' yards to protect from disease and mites. But bees can fly over two miles in any direction, so, particularly in the lowlands, we can't always control their choice of dining destination. Even with careful planning there isn't much we can do about bad weather, unexpected spraying, ants, vandals and bears. We do what we can.

During winter and spring, on Sundays, we sell honey at one or two farmers markets in Seattle. From May to November you'll find us at five or six markets a week. Often it feels like too many valuable hours away from our five acres in the forest by the river, time away from tending the bees, and too many hours standing on concrete. And always too many hours of freeway driving.

Nevertheless, we look forward to the rewards of market days. While we sell, we share our lives with city dwellers and visitors from across the country and around the world. We educate customers about different types of honey, bees, pollination, the environment, the many facets of beekeeping, struggles to ensure the survival of bees and latest scandals of the international honey trade. Encouraging neophyte backyard beekeepers, we show photographs, tell tales of beekeeping in the web of nature and cross-pollinate with other farmers. An always-fascinating cross-section of people in turn share their own tales. Many customers are immigrants who treasure honey and other hive products for use as medicine, especially Russians, Eastern Europeans, and East Africans, for whom honey is a valuable item on their shopping list.

We love our customers. As farmers, our connection with the people we feed is essential. Except for the venue of local farmers' markets, most farmers, and in particular 'agri-biz' corporate serfs, have lost that connection, with the result of less than optimal—and often horrifying—methods of food production. And with the ever increasing, seemingly unstoppable corporate/pharmaceutical globalization of the food industry, the farmer/consumer connection becomes even more tenuous.

Some farmers won't eat their own commercial crops because of pesticides and only eat produce from small organic 'kitchen' patches in their own backyard. If these farmers met and conversed with their customers face to face, would they continue to grow toxic crops? I don't think so. But the farmers must witness what people buy when they walk through the supermarket produce aisle. I know that if I don't have the time, or a place, to grow my own food, I do want to know what practices, processes and permutations affect what I eat.

Although most people lack the opportunity, the knowledge, or the desire to grow their own food, they should have access to talk to and support the farmers who provide their nourishment. People living in the Pacific Northwest are fortunate to have easy access to so many farmers who sell quality organic products through CSAs (Community Supported Agricultural programs), co-ops and local farmers markets.

At markets where we sell, we are blessed with an endless supply of fresh organic local produce from other growers, with more and more exotic varieties available each year, as well as fresh baked bread, organic cheese, eggs, meat and fish. And we have honey to trade.

☼

Once a year, in spring, we travel south to buy new bees to replace those that succumbed to old age, disease, hard work and the rigors of winter. We also buy young queens to replace old or failing royalty.

Today we're in southern Oregon to rendezvous with a California beekeeper and bee breeder, Bob, who has brought his hives temporarily to the Ashland area for orchard pollination. He will sell us our new bees.

A dusting of hilltop snow deepens the early morning hush above the wide valley of fruit farms west of Ashland. Below the slopes of white-brushed hills, thousands and thousands of acres of white petals float like a Japanese dream over rows of blooming pear, apple and cherry trees. Between every second tree propane burners stand like sentries, ready to be lit at the slightest hint of frost.

We pull into an orchard. Every hundred yards, a deep hum rises from clusters of white beehives filled with thousands of immigrant worker bees visiting from California for pollination. But no bees are out flying yet this chilly morning.

Standing beside the small travel trailer that the beekeepers call home during pollination, weatherworn Bob and his smiling wife greet us.

"Bees're ready to go. Poured sixty boxfuls yesterday. Heavy hives this year, no problem. Shook a few extra frames too." Always generous with the bees he sells us, Bob often throws in an extra half-pound per box. And yes, the bees *are* poured into their travel boxes through a funnel when they're shaken from their frames.

The humming wooden travel boxes, each slightly larger than a child's lunch box, screened on either side, are neatly stacked and ready to go. Inside each container, bees hang in a ball around a caged queen and cling to each other in a fuzzy heaving mass. Docile, and happy to keep their queen company in the cool morning, the bees are ignorant of the long journey that lies ahead.

Bob, his wife, Roy and I make a chain to unload last year's empty containers before carefully stacking the new boxes of bees in the back of our pickup. Stray bees buzzing around outside the boxes don't bother us as we work and none of us wear veil or gloves. The loading is swift and uneventful, with minimal escapees. Before long, our little red Toyota vibrates with whir and purr, every inch under the canopy filled with the contented humming cargo and we're ready for the journey home with this year's shipment of young bees. At approximately ten thousand bees to a pound, with sixty boxes, with three or four pounds per box, that's close to two million bees. With two million stingers. An impressive number of armed insects confined in a small space. We will make every effort to be as kind to them as possible. Insurrection is not an option.

Along with the sixty boxes full of young worker bees and a queen, we take twenty-five extra queens in separate mesh-walled wooden cages the size of cigarette lighters. The queens get the royal treatment of traveling up front between us on the seat of the cab, calling to each other with high clear peeping sounds before they settle down for the ride. I wonder what they're saying, and if anyone has studied peep translation. Are they communicating with us? Or just with each other? Would they like us to know what they're saying?

On the road home, in predictably unpredictable April weather, sullen gray/black clouds tear open in a drenching storm of hail. Traffic slows to a crawl as ice balls ping and bounce off the slushy highway. Hailstones pile in mounds on the shiny asphalt. Almost immediately the hard white granules melt like sugar to a slick coat of frosting. Then within minutes a diluted sun peeks out and numinous rainbows splash the damp countryside. We drive through six, yes six, sudden hailstorms as we drive north along I-5 past Eugene and Portland to the Puget Sound, always careful to leave a wide space between our pickup and the cars in front. We pray that unknowing cars behind have the sense to do the same.

The bees don't complain while icy hail cools the canopy roof, but when we're stuck in an hour-long traffic jam in a bright sun break, steam rises from the roof and the anxious volume of buzz rises as fast as the temperature. We're grateful for frequent exits where we can spray the boxes with water.

At rest areas and gas stations, an entourage of escaped bees floats, weaves, and circles a halo around the mysterious-sounding red pickup. Curious bystanders stop and stare.

"Look Mommy! Look at bees! Bees, bees!"

"No Joey! Get back here!" shrieks Mom. She rushes to grab her curious three-year-old as he heads straight for the Toyota. Tight-jeaned teenagers squeal and giggle by the convenience store door.

Not everyday do people see a cloud of hovering bees dancing around a vehicle by a gas pump. Big commercial beekeeping operations–which contract thousands of hives for pollination across the USA–load 18-wheelers with hundreds of hives, throw a fine net over the whole buzzing shipment and transport under cover of darkness. At the start of pollination season watch for nighttime bee-laden semis on interstates! Especially if you're on a sharp curve in a spring snowstorm.

Driving straight up I-5, with only quick pit stops to cool the bees and fill up with gas, we arrive on our five acres by the Hood Canal as late afternoon sun fades behind tall firs around our forest clearing. We're relieved to be home. Disaster scenarios spun from our potentially catastrophic cargo are beyond what I care to imagine, even though they would make exciting reading.

CHAPTER 2

RIVER LAND

A POSSE OF bees veers left from an orchard hive to hunt fresh nectar and pollen hiding in dew-soaked blossom. Hurrying to beat the next April shower, I join them in their hunt for the hidden promise and surprise of spring, hungry for exceptional moments of revelation. Across the forest clearing, a veil of mist evaporates, leaving a quilt of shimmering webs that drift and sparkle from fir to fir. Already my thirst for surprise and wonder has been rewarded.

My shiny yellow rubber boots, invaders in a land of muted shades, swish through damp grass to the edge of a forested hillside that drops to the Tahuya River valley below. The Tahuya River, pronounced 'Tahooya,' an Indian word for 'meeting place', flows south from Lake Tahuya in Kitsap County, through the Tahuya peninsula to the North Shore of the Hood Canal. Our overgrown five-acre riverside haven lies half way down the Tahuya peninsula in the middle of the Tahuya State Forest. The Tahuya peninsula hangs like a big toe from the Kitsap peninsula, which juts northward on the eastern edge of the Olympic peninsula. Living on a peninsula, on a peninsula, on a peninsula is like living at the center of a maze. Few uninvited people venture to where a missed turn might lead to hours of frustrating, though scenic, driving.

I hike the winding river trail. A third of the way down the steep slope I pay my respects to the Guardian of the Forest: a weather-rotted wood burl, shaped like a horse head gargoyle with a ceremonial hanging-moss hairdo, who grins at the end of a broken branch sticking out from an old stump. I imagine the Guardian to be a wild shamanic horse who guards the threshold to mysteries of the wilderness, a forest spirit watching over hillside and river, gatekeeper to a supernatural world where connections and agreements are made, where gifts are freely given and received and where resonance embraces all life forms. Bowing my head slightly in his direction, I trust the shaggy-maned Guardian to protect our peaceful forest home.

Further down the river trail I pause where beaded-bone lichen encrusts a branch with miniature ochre cups that glow like a science fiction city. Lichen—a synergy of flora and fauna in mutually beneficial collaboration—thrives in the absence of pollution in this dripping, organic land, as does any plant or animal with an affinity for water, including me. Rain power blesses the land with energy. Any open-hearted person who enters the lush forestland gains easy access to the living/dying, growing/fading essence of water, wood, leaf and lichen.

Reaching the valley floor, 150 feet below our clearing, I turn south onto a long-unused logging road running parallel to the river under a tangle of alder, fir, big-leaf and vine maple. From the old logging track I cut left to my favorite, and very private, river beach.

Although the middle of the Tahuya River marks the eastern boundary of our property, each year the main channel veers half-a-dozen feet to the east or to the west and the boundary shifts, as fluctuating and as fluid as the river's winding course to the Hood Canal. Gently sloped pebbles at the river's edge submerge yearly under winter floods, but after the water subsides in spring, smooth pebbles welcome me to sit, watch, listen and meditate undisturbed away from the business of beekeeping. Although Roy, his teenage son Ian, and I are the only humans who visit this stretch of river, we share the valley with eagle, deer, beaver, river otter, coyote, bear, salmon and dozens of other small creatures, birds and insects—including, of course, honeybees from the hives we keep around our home.

I love the river in all her moods and constant change. The river is my guide, my ally and mentor. Today I stand still and quiet on the beach, slow my breath, and lose myself to the soothing burble of water as time and thought melt like this morning's evaporating mists. My mind slips easily into shimmering reverie. Many stopped minutes later my thought-mind reawakens, changes course and slides smoothly back to the presence of the river's ways.

I scan the damp air for bees at the river this morning searching for a drink of water or suck of nectar from an early blossom, but don't see a single black and yellow flier. Today the bees prefer the warmth of home.

Along the riverbank, new shoots of spring–lusty rush spears, grass and sedge–elbow through washed skeletons of moldy straw-colored reeds. Two mallards drift downstream from a bend to the north. I am right in their line of travel. They brake fast, not expecting company, especially the large human variety, and in unison turn tail, splash and paddle frantically against the central current to a sheltered pool under the far bank. The alert male eyes me cautiously, floating guard while the female goes back to dabbling for a nibble. The metallic hues of the drake's green head, his stark white neck ring and the contrasting shades of the drab brown female make me wonder about when human males are more flamboyant than females. Perhaps fancy-dancers of American Indian traditions or indigenous cultures who paint or tattoo their bodies to attract a mate?

Dividing our river frontage into 'north of the logjam' and 'south of the logjam', a chaotic jumble of forest debris blockades the river like a giant beaver dam. But I insult beaver by any comparison to their meticulous construction and creative symmetry, for the logjam is neither. The logjam is a twined madness of mangled branches, trunks and toppled whole trees. Anarchy rules in a tantrum thrown by Mother Nature.

From late spring to early winter the logjam lazes like a chaotic sprawling statue, then November rains flush from saturated clouds and the wall of debris invents a whole new persona. Winter water pounces down the valley, grabbing trees and branches, tossing its prey to the many-limbed monster of the logjam. New legs, arms, toes and crooked fingers stick out at crazy angles. Weatherworn cedar logs, hemlock and fir pile against fallen alder and maple, their roots washed bare by the suck of water. Last winter, the hungry river gobbled a long section of low bank, throwing a large alder and a fir to slam into the untidy wall of disintegrating wood.

The logjam is never an obstacle for the persistent river. Water sneaks and insinuates, rushes and pushes to find new pathways to flow under, around and through the woody barrier. Water gushes and pours over smooth-washed wood, jagged sticks, stems, snags and snarls. The flow will not be dammed. No wonder rivers represent the natural flow of life. Always, if unhampered by man, rivers will find a way.

Every winter, not only the logjam, but the whole geography of the river course rebirths. New beaches rise up. Old beaches vanish. Puddles become ponds. Old ponds become muddy dips, virgin silt for pioneering sprouts. The river babbles and rushes. The river slurps, cavorts and slithers around water-gouged banks. The river sculpts and molds the vessel of her tireless flow.

I think of the journey of first drops sprung from the river source and wonder if any of the same water flowing through our land reaches the Pacific Ocean beyond the Hood Canal and the Straits of Juan De Fuca. Someday I might play message and bottle to find out.

Today, in late spring, behind the resting logjam, sprays of fir and fern and beaver-peeled sticks float on a deep pool. Are the sticks a stockpile of future building materials? Are they discards from a work zone, not the right fit or shape for a dam? Or are they licked-clean meal bones? Each day, as beaver thin a tangle of vine maple and baby alder, more tooth-marked stumps jut like sharpened medieval barricades from the riverbank. As if to keep pace with the beavers' voracious appetites, shoots race to grow back after the perpetual pruning. Beyond the logjam, woven brown, white and green twigs shore-up the front of a pool where beaver build a low wall, one stick at a time, to protect a future lodge for a growing family. The beavers' main lodge hides further upstream in a flooded valley of meandering ponds.

I am almost always gifted a peeled walking stick from the legacy of bark snacks that pattern the banks. But even though several beaver call this valley their home, I have never seen one. I respect their privacy and won't disturb their nocturnal foraging and construction. At twilight I leave the valley to the natives of river-land and seldom visit the river at night. This year I'd like to meet a beaver, if only to thank him for his latest gift of a walking stick.

A bitter smell rises from woods west of the river. I dive into the woods to follow the smell to its source, a sour black water bog of rotting leaves, scum and fallen alder catkins where untidy clumps of skunk cabbage thrust fluorescent beacons into the half-light. Native Americans roasted and dried skunk cabbage roots then ground them into flour. Leaves of the primordial plant were used to wrap salmon and other foods when cooking over a fire pit. But here's a warning. Don't eat the leaves! They contain a nasty mouth-stinging acid (a tip from a friend who immediately regretted a reckless sample).

A red-legged frog startles me when he plops off a log into a dusty bed of leaves; his mottled back painted a near perfect camouflage, his reddish belly and under-legs well hidden from view. He doesn't shift a muscle, but half-hooded eyes that shine with the light of pure intelligence betray his disguise. He squats motionless, every ounce of awareness poised for escape. If amphibians have emotions, then this frog's emotions must be on overload when confronted by this enormous creature who could snuff out his woodland life in an instant. How would I behave in a similar situation? I hope I never have to find out.

I move first. Perhaps the frog thinks he fooled this giant into believing he's dead undergrowth when I turn back through the woods. I slink away with more stealth than before. Encounter with the tangible awareness of a small creature assessing potential danger nudges me to a quieter space within where my breath slows and movements arise with a gentler flow.

Along maple-treed slopes beside the swamp, trillium, the first woodland flowers, poke through decaying leaves, announcing spring with pure and graceful lines of three white petals and three simple leaves. Trillium, an endangered species from loss of habitat and decimated by over-zealous harvesting by wild-crafters for medicinal properties, may wait up to fifteen years before the first flower opens, but rhizomes as old as seventy years have been found. If the flowers are picked, the plants might not grow back.

A loud buzzing insect flies into my hair, bounces off and lands disoriented on a mossy twig. I am as startled as he. The scarlet wings, legs and head of the red bark beetle shine a bright contrast to the dull grayish-green moss. The beetles usually hide in the dark shelter of loose bark and fallen logs. Perhaps this one was blinded by daylight before crashing into me. Or maybe he mistook my hair for the shelter of fuzzy lichen.

☼

Well satisfied with today's ramble in my paradise river valley, I hike back up the trail to our half-acre vegetable garden at the north end of the clearing.

Years ago, when I first moved to the Pacific Northwest from the Sawtooth mountains of Idaho, where nurturing any plant to fruition was a monumental task, I was amazed by how much time I spent doing just the opposite–persuading unwanted plants to not grow in the garden. My first attempt at northwest horticulture in a Portland backyard ended as a jungle of runaway nasturtiums and far too many pounds of tomatoes.

13

I am a lazy gardener. I sew seeds, then leave nature to do whatever she pleases until I must rush to the rescue of choking seedlings. No neatly weeded beds. Wilderness rampages between rows. My excuse is that bugs will gorge on the green excess and retreat with a full belly before discovery of my cultivated treasures.

Today the vegetable garden shines with raindrop jewels. Gemstones on grass blades. Crystals on kale. Pearls on bent garlic leaves.

Recent steady rain has left the ground cold, heavy and waterlogged, not yet time to prepare the soil for vegetable planting. But some plants have flourished in the moisture, especially moss, chickweed and grass.

So much garlic sprang from last year's unharvested bulbs that I won't plant more this year. I already transplanted a fifty-foot raised bed with shoots and gave away a bucketful of starts. Unexpected patches of kale, re-seeded from the year before last, shoot wildly from every corner. I like that. Volunteer kale makes an easy choice for dinner greens. Vagabond kale pops up between stones in the walkway to the workshop/honey-house, and sturdiest of all, a giant rogue towers over a corner of the compost pile. Nearby, another plant also suckles from the potent pile: wrinkled rhubarb leaves unfurl from scarlet stalks like large golfing umbrellas.

While Roy prunes apple trees in the orchard, I finish digging a small flowerbed beside the sunny honey house/workshop wall. I rip out fistfuls of crabgrass and shake valuable soil from impossibly long invading runners that creep underground eighteen sneaky inches. I have foiled their plot for an unexpected uprising! As self-appointed commander-in-chief of this future flower-land I'll host a civilized assortment of pretty, domesticated catalog flowers from seeds expected soon in the mail. I victoriously lay claim to and control over this little patch of earth. At least for now.

CHAPTER 3

HIVING

THOUSANDS OF hungry field bees, residents of seventy over-wintered hives, crawl over blossom in our sunny bee yard at the toe of the Hood Canal. A handful of guard bees, vigilant but mellow, zwoop and zoom to scrutinize two figures in white bee suits who just invaded their territory, but soon lose interest when we don't approach their homes. The beekeepers' focus today is not with the over-wintered hives, but with the construction of thirty new hives to shelter recent arrivals from California.

Our materials for assembling thirty hives: a complexity of bottom boards, green painted deep hive boxes, frames fitted with wax foundation, screen boards, moisture boards, feeder rims, and lids for each hive. Many tall stacks of each.

After positioning bottom boards in staggered rows beside the old over-wintered hives, we run up and down the rows, then up and down the rows again, and again, to distribute the rest of the construction materials. After delivering all the components, plus a break to observe the other hard working yard residents, we raise the new housing development piece by piece. The busy residents neither pay attention to us nor take time out to watch us work. The new bees wait patiently in the back of the little red pickup.

Several hours of steady work, and several more breaks for bee watching later, the thirty sage colored hives are ready and it's time to introduce the recent arrivals to their new environment. As daylight fades, Roy shakes worker bees from the travel boxes into waiting honeycomb foundation inside the hive boxes. The furry insects flip and tumble down the frames. When all the workers from each travel box are hived, I gently wedge the small queen cage between frames close to the seething mounds of bees. Lured by the familiar scent of their queen's magnetic pheromones, the bees immediately scurry to attend to her every need.

The best time to hive bees is late in the day. Overnight they'll clean themselves and set up housekeeping in their new living quarters. They don't waste time. By tomorrow morning the colony will be established and the bees eager for first flights to scout for nectar. And pollen. After that, the queen will be laying and the bee population will expand like everything else this spring.

As the sun sinks below the southern end of the Olympic Mountains a chill breeze creeps across marshy land at the end of the Hood Canal, reminding us that it is still April as we leave our brand new subdivision of sage green hives.

☼

The overcast, nondescript day is perfect for setting up more hives and hiving the rest of the bees. Twenty-eight packages of bees remain trapped in their traveling boxes, and although the bees have cans of sugar syrup for food, after two days captivity they're eager to leave cramped quarters, spread their wings and feast on real nectar. And they're ready for a bathroom break.

For the first time this year Roy fires up his old white propane-powered flatbed truck equipped with a boom and mechanical lifter for moving hives. After loading the long bed with the buzzing packages, beehive boxes, miscellaneous construction materials and fence making equipment, we head north to establish a bee yard on the west side of the Hood Canal. An hour's drive later we cross the Hood Canal floating bridge near the mouth of the Canal, then turn southwest into the Olympic foothills. North of Quilcene we turn onto a logging road by Snow Creek and unlock a heavy orange metal gate. We like locked gates. For several years we have leased keys from the same timber management company for access to clear cuts that provide acres and acres of prime flower pasture.

The logging road meanders uphill into the foothills for a couple of miles to a recent clear cut. At twenty-five hundred feet above sea level we pull over on a small level platform, a no longer used logging turnaround with a three-hundred-and-sixty degree view, where we kept hives last year. The bees will thrive with the all-day sun and an easy flight path in every direction. A panoramic view sweeps across miles of rolling wooded hills and valleys with lower elevation pale green slopes of alder and maple dissolving to higher dark coniferous forest; a beautiful green layered landscape except for a bad haircut collage of clear-cuts in ragged stages of re-growth.

But for beekeepers, omnipresent clear-cuts have unexpected benefits. Sunny logged-off slopes in the Northwest are ideal for the germination of fluffy fireweed seeds. The first plant to grow back after the devastation of a forest fire, fireweed was originally given that name for its connection with forest fires, not because of the brilliant fiery slopes of pink summer blossom. Acres of fireweed transform barren land into bee heaven a year or two after slopes have been shaved. And fireweed yields prize-winning honey.

In a good hot year, when summer temperatures rise consistently above 70 degrees, fireweed flowers pump out nectar that the bees turn to a clear, light and sometimes almost transparent honey. But for the last two years, cool and rainy Northwest weather spoiled the flowering season and even though flowers splashed the hillsides, little nectar rose through the stems, and the honey harvest was disappointing. We keep our fingers crossed for a summer ahead of hot August days.

Last year, despite the security of locked gates, hives were vandalized at three separate locations. This was one of them.

During hunting season, before we brought bees down from the foothills for winter, a trigger-happy jerk destroyed half-a-dozen hives by gunfire.

The vandalism happened shortly before Roy arrived to check hives at the site. The air was black with enraged bees when he reached the yard. Bees poured from splintered gashes in the wooden hive walls. Bullets had ripped holes through one hive to the next and beyond. Dead and dying bees littered the ground. Honey trickled down the sides of shattered boxes as robber bees from untargeted hives zoomed in to the sticky mess for a free lunch. Distraught bees from the broken hives circled in a bewildered frenzy.

Upset and saddened, Roy left the devastation to follow the monster tire tracks of a four-wheel-drive vehicle. At a locked gate, skid marks indicated that the malicious intruder made a quick turnaround and took off cross-country in a rush, looking for another way out. Hopefully the vandal's hasty exit included at least a handful of irate bees with revenge stamped on their stripes. Maybe that's why the jerk was anxious to leave. Fast.

There was nothing we could do. The timber company told Roy they had no extra staff to patrol the huge acreage, complained about damage to their own property, and warned that vandalism was common, especially during hunting season.

This year perhaps we should post a sign that reads "This Area Under Surveillance!" even if only the surveillance of innocent, well-armed bees. With current technological security systems, perhaps someone might just believe they're being watched by a relay system of satellite surveillance in the mountains. A solar powered camera would work as well, but then that might also invite target practice.

Today, at this platform in the Quilcene foothills, we'll first erect an electric fence to protect the apiary from other animals, specifically the large black furry kind. In addition to the danger of human vandalism, this is bear country. A bear's ungracious table manners can wreak instant havoc as he rips apart boxes and frames to feast on young bee larvae.

However, I can easily understand and sympathize with a bear destroying a hive for food and survival. It is far more difficult to understand the senseless act of a callous human. At least we stand a chance to protect colonies from a hungry bear, but not from a gun-toting idiot. Perhaps, if the vandal had been more familiar with the value of pollinators, and educated about the intricate, complex, amazing life and essential goodness and value of bees, he might have thought twice before using hives for target practice. Wishful thinking.

Roy drives a metal stake into the hard ground at ten-foot intervals around the perimeter of the yard. We walk three times around the outside, winding rows of wire around the stakes, leaving three hooked ends open for easy entry to the yard.

An electric fence, on its own, is little deterrent to a thick-furred bear. The small jolt would be no more than a nettle sting, and the hungry bear would breach the barrier before the next small shock. So Roy came up with an ingenious idea. He attaches four cracked-open sardine cans to the top wire, one on each side of the yard facing outward. Bears love the smell of fish. Their snout searches for the source of the stinky smell; their tongue reaches out, and YIKES! After one electrifying tongue-tip taste they stumble away fast on their stubby legs, shaken but not much harmed, with no desire to return. If only we could come up with a comparable plan to deter macho gun-drunk humans. Maybe cans of beer?

We work fast to assemble twenty-five new hives. A repeat of bottom board, screen board, hive body, frames with foundation, feeder rim, moisture board, hive cover and a baggie of feed. After a while it gets to be a rhythm. We set the hives in uneven rows facing south for the entrances to catch direct sun for the longest hours. When the hive bodies are ready, we move down the staggered rows from hive to hive, shake bees from their travel boxes, then release a queen into each new bee-palace.

Fireweed is still weeks away from blossoming, and flowers at this hilly elevation bloom after those in the valleys below, offering minimal bee forage in the immediate neighborhood. But bees fly more than two miles in any direction, and it is not far to wing to a nearby flowering valley where maple tassels droop with nectar, and red currant and salmonberry accent lower woodland slopes. Plus, within a month, hillsides will be overrun by acres of nectar-sweet Evergreen and Himalayan blackberry blossom.

Roy hooks shut the bear fence and connects the wires to a battery. As darkness falls we leave the construction site to our new tenants who will emerge in morning light to a landscape very different from the hot California valley of their birth. Our hardy bees are descendants of Carneolan stock, originally from the Austrian Alps, and we have Russian queens, so even though the bees were born in California, their ancestral cold-weather genes will help them adapt easily to this cooler climate.

A hundred yards from one of our bee yards, a tall stand-alone cedar grows close to the Union River bridge. Last fall we often watched a pair of mated bald eagles perched in the old tree as they surveyed wide sweeps of wetlands at the toe of the Hood Canal. Pleased with the panoramic hunting vista and promising meal potential, the birds began construction of a nest in the ragged branches.

Now, six months later, an impressive eagle stands guard at the top of the snag, while the white head of his mate peers over the rim of the newly built nest of heavy sticks. We're thrilled that they've chosen a visible location where we can watch progress of their expanding family. Last winter, silvery screeches of a mated pair, perhaps the same pair, echoed for months along our backyard stretch of the Tahuya River.

But we wonder why the mated eagles have chosen to raise a family so close to town. Do they fear people less since becoming an endangered species? Perhaps the increased salmon count in the Union River below decided their choice. Last year more salmon than usual returned to spawn in nearby creeks, a result of salmon eggs released four years ago in the stream below the nest. Bald eagles have made a remarkable comeback in the lower 48 states since 1963 when less than 500 mated pairs were recorded. Now, with over 10,000 and steadily rising, there are rumors that they will no longer receive protection as an endangered species. I hope that honeybees will make a similar comeback.

CHAPTER 4

SPRING WOODLANDS

SILKEN GRAY cloaks dark firs at the edge of the backyard. Rain has fallen since early morning. Not a pounding downpour, not April showers, but a steady slow-fall of wet that splatters with a rhythmic pop, splash and occasional hammer of drops and drips. Just as the Inuit have dozens of words for snow, Pacific Northwest life prompts an elaborate vocabulary of adjectives, adverbs and metaphors for the many moods and nuance of rain, one of my favorites a line from a friend of mine: 'the air hung with so much moisture that it threatened to be water'.

The wind picks up speed, sways fir and hemlock branches and rattles loose windows. Wet-feathered flyers warble in the trees despite the less-than-perfect weather. I follow their disregard for the falling rain and dive into the land of wet. Raining or not, plant and animal life refuse to hold back the vital energy of this season of growth and change. The energy of water both intensifies and blurs the urgency of spring.

Shortly before Roy bought this land, large trees were logged from the hilltop clearing and he was left to uproot the remaining stumps. At the river trailhead a bulldozed pile waves amputated limbs in the air like giant extracted teeth. Some stumps measure three feet across where the blade fell. Not old growth, but large enough. How huge those trees must have been in their living splendor. How fantastic this landscape must have been before the forests were cut and re-cut.

The loggers spared smaller fir, pine, and hemlock. Some of these conifers have grown to over 100 feet and the woods underneath have filled out with alder, vine maple, cascara, willow and cottonwood. The rich ecosystem regenerates with impressive speed.

I am grateful the decomposing stump pile wasn't burned. Plants and wildlife have reclaimed the heap. Nature reuses and recycles and reuses and recycles again. Lichens and fungus coat damp walls inside the half-rotted roots where dozens of small creatures and insects maintain every inch of the hidden hollows, cracks and caves for sheltering burrows, condos and nests. Today only a couple of spiders dawdle outside in the wet. Caches of chipmunk and squirrel food—pinecones and half-eaten nuts—scatter the hollowed-out trunks. Pink single-petal flowers spray from red-stemmed huckleberry hovering over a moss cushion on the stump pile while, below, buds of evergreen huckleberry bulge pale pink, ready to burst into bloom for our bees to suck and turn to smoothest honey. Delicate yellow round-leaved violets cascade from the mossy island.

I nod to the Guardian at the threshold of the forest.

Fir needles, soggy skeletal leaves and alder catkins pave the river trail. Bushes, needles and twigs either side of the path glisten slick and wet. Thigh-high evergreen salal protects hillsides along the river valley from erosion. But salal itself is not protected. A growing number of brush pickers harvest salal leaves from local forests. The leaves stay fresh looking for days, a prized commodity for florists nationwide. At least the salal on our property is safe.

In fresh smelling woodlands of mid April buds race to open timid petals and wave pollen-dusted stamens. Moment to moment, a transformation. Overnight, pushy nettles shoot up two inches with an armory of tiny hairs and at least two new

23

leaves. Horsetail ferns rush like rockets toward the light. When dinosaurs roamed the planet, giant horsetail grew as tall as trees. More recently, horsetail was sought as a springtime vegetable for coastal Indians and I've used the plant for scouring pots while camping. Now, whenever possible, horsetail is ripped out as a noxious weed, a fall from grace from a shady haven for dinosaurs to an unwanted weed sometimes called 'devil guts'.

From a high fir lookout, a raucous Stellar's jay with tufted head and blue body squawks to the neighborhood that a human in yellow rubber boots is out and about.

A siege of white, gray and green lichens presses against twigs and trunks in a fairytale setting for woodland spirits. Usnea longissima—also known as Methuselah's Beard—hangs in curtains. Pale hair-like strands, some as long as ten foot, loop and drip and sway and billow with the delicacy of woven elfin lace. Valuable for antibacterial properties, usnea is effective as an antibiotic for sinus infections. The inner thread is an immune system stimulant while the outer covering is antibiotic. I've learned to identify usnea by wetting a strand and pulling it apart to see if the inner core has a stretchy, rubber-band-like quality, though I've yet to test its medicinal claims.

Salmonberry flowers entice honeybees, bumblebees and passing hummingbirds. Bright magenta petals splash a backdrop of electric green foliage; skunk cabbage yellow flower sheaths jostle up from muddy hollows; a tangle of storm-felled alder branches sprout olive-green crinkled Shibori-like leaves for one last year of growth. My mind whirls from the feast of texture and color as I brush through the sprouting undergrowth of spring.

Cedar stumps on the valley slopes conjure ghosts of former grandeur. Dwarfed to six-to-ten foot stumps by hungry saws more than half a century ago, they still stand proud after weathering decades of rain and storm. The original towering biomass has evolved into a complex ecosystem around the cedar spirit stumps. A crazy-quilt mosaic of moss, lichen, bushy fern, salal and huckleberry sprout from a decaying mulch of alder and maple leaves blanketing the crowns. The crumbling inner core of a stump, chewed by hidden termite armies, pours out a fountain of red dust and quietly turns it to nutrient rich soil. The disintegrating outer cedar bark rots far more slowly.

Cedar, not affected by water, takes dozens of years to break down, making it a valuable sought-after material for canoes and roof shingles. And expensive homes. Demand far exceeds supply for the strong, light, sweet-fragranced wood, and now cedar is only harvested by special permit. I've heard that cedar poaching is common. Recently, I drove past a broken gate in a timber company forest and guessed that the heavy metal gate had been destroyed for illegal access to high-dollar-value timber. Experienced cedar rustlers can break in, cut trees, load out with lightning speed, then drive to a neighboring state to sell the cedar with few questions asked.

A shifting chorus of frog-song accompanies my rainy wander around ponds by the river and I wonder if one of the ribbits comes from the red-legged frog I met a few days ago. I'm sure he remembers my heavy tread. Eavesdropping on staccato broadcasts croaked in rhythm with the dripping afternoon, I'm constantly amazed that as small a creature as a frog can reverberate such a loud sound. The language of croaks comforts me, knowing that these amphibians still thrive in their fast disappearing habitat.

Dripping furry bracken sprouts beside the path. Tender nettles poke through a sandy patch by the river beach. Soon, four-foot bracken fronds will hide the forest floor; nettles will be six-foot tall, assuring ever more river and woodland privacy that I'm especially thankful for when I river-lounge in summer.

A 'bear tree' grows by the overgrown disused logging road parallel to the river. About fifteen years ago a black bear claimed this territory when he gouged six inches deep, and a third of the way around, the lower trunk of the tall fir. Despite the deep gash, the inner core still grows strong, and the blackened wound expands along with the tree, now almost three foot in diameter. Two years ago I watched a bear cross a nearby forest road. A week later, two more lumbered in front of our truck for fifty yards. But bears avoid our small community and haven't been seen on our land for more than ten years, though they roam neighboring forests and undoubtedly know about the sweet honey and larval temptations of our beehives. Our half-wild dog, Zap, with his threatening growl and rough bark, guards the beehives well.

High water floods a usually dry creek by the river and rivulets have molded hillocks into small islands. Spiky sedge and reeds struggle to hold their own in a swift spring current. I cross to a mid-river island on a fallen cedar trunk. Beneath the weatherworn bridge, water churns and wrestles over rapids, pushes through a narrow gap, froths, foams and gallops like a rodeo bull released from its pen. Raindrops splash endless bubble patterns of drift and pop on the swirling central current.

On the beach, wet pebbles gleam with every shade of gray accented by jade, red jasper and smooth white marble. A backwater lazes idly, sheltered by overhanging branches. Drips collect on twigs, trickle down, splash and melt silently through the liquid surface with overlapping, sinuous concentric circles that glide across the pool. The water-skin mesmerizes with a quivering kinetic dance of ever-expanding motion.

Lulled to dreamtime by the dripping world and the swoosh of the river, I turn my face to the sky and close my eyes, lost in an eyelid trance of rippling twined rings. Rain, falling softly now, brushes my forehead with a caress, trickles over my eyebrows and slides in silken rivulets down my cheeks.

CHAPTER 5

FOREST TRAILS

I HIKE UP the violet-lined driveway, leave our five acres, turn left and walk past the overgrown driveway of the five-acre neighboring property. Absentee owners visit the land once a year to mow the driveway and a small clearing hidden behind a wall of trees. We like the privacy of no immediate neighbors.

Three hundred yards to the south, a State Forest trail crosses our community access road. West of the road, the trail runs through logged land where spindly firs and undergrowth struggle to grow back. After crossing a bridge over a small creek, the trail, which I've named the Open Trail, winds several miles through another logged area, ending at a lake. East of the road, the path that I call the Tall Trees Trail, disappears into a thick forest of second growth trees. Naming territory must be inherent in human nature. For me it gives the pleasure of familiarity, belonging, honoring, and a secret sense of owning, even though it is not mine to own. I wonder if animals name their trails too, as in 'Leads-to-the-Chicken-House-Trail'.

The muddy path of the Open Trail is badly chewed and rutted. Dust and mud splatter vegetation for five feet on either side of the track. Brown spotted leaves hang weakly from stunted, withered and yellowed undergrowth as plants choke

27

and die, victims of the ever-increasing number of dirt bikes that race along the trail.

Hundreds of miles of trails wind through the State Forest that surrounds our small community, making it a prime western Washington destination for dirt bike riders. Hikers, horses and mountain bikes used to enjoy the trails, but now dirt bikes and the latest addition, the four-wheel quad, hold the trails hostage. On weekends, for recreation, dozens of colorful leather-clad riders, alien space parasites stuck to shiny chrome hosts, zip to and fro through the forest. We're usually away selling at markets on weekends, but on weekdays, when I find time to wander away from our five acres, the trails are quiet and the land rests from the desecrating vibrations of the noisy machines.

While wandering through woods by the river I'm often aware of the damage my heavy tread through the undergrowth inflicts and don't fool myself into thinking that I have the stealth of a deer, or the wisdom of indigenous people who lived for centuries in balance and harmony with nature. When my feet tread the same path too many times, my tracks leave a scar on the earth. I am careful to either stay on an already well-worn path or differ my route through the woods with each exploration.

The word 'recreation' has taken on a life of its own. The way we 're' 'create' more and more involves equipment and machinery. The meaning of recreation–'to impart fresh life to'– might apply to the bike riders but definitely does not apply to their dusty assault on the forest trails and surrounding vegetation. But dirt bikers need recreation after days of an eight-to-five routine, and I always hold the hope that excursions into this delicate landscape will open a window to an appreciation of nature with quieter, gentler ways of enjoying the forest while there still are forests. Maybe this is just wishful thinking.

Half-a-dozen tall trees stand awkward and alone. When loggers razed the land they left one solitary tree per acre as marker trees. Two years ago a hillside west of the Open Trail was logged. For one long agonizing month I woke each dawn to whining saws, grinding machinery, the groan, creak and crash of a falling tree, then a silent moment before another tree fell target to a blade. My body tensed with every whine until I'd pull a blanket up over my ears and retreat to a gentler land of sleep and dream.

I turn my attention from sad memories and return to the present, to the ground beside the path. With more light from the recent clear-cut, vegetation by the Open Trail grows faster than on our five acres and already pretty pink urn shaped flowers of manzanita are in bloom. Simple wild strawberry blossoms embroider banks; buds bulge on huckleberry and wild rhodies.

After hiking back along the trail, I cross our access road and dive into the darkness of Tall Trees Trail. Year round, whenever I enter the big-treed forest I can hear it whisper to me: "Go within, go within. We trees have been here so much longer than you. Be still. Be quiet. Listen to the wisdom within these forests and within you." I wish that everyone who enters these woods would stand still for a few minutes, lean back against an ancient trunk and hear the same whispering of the trees.

Lush moss carpets sprawl across the dim-lit forest floor, drape disintegrating stumps, swell wavelike around serpentine roots, clothe ancient nurse logs and bury fallen branches with tufted green velvet.

The Tall Trees Trail forest will be clear-cut soon. Whenever I walk by neon-colored plastic streamers fluttering from tagged trees I'm reminded of the impending destruction and must resist the temptation to disappear the ominous ribbons. Contracts have been written and any morning we will again wake to logging trucks and the whine of saws. Every time I drive home past the forest I am grateful to see that the trees still grow tall. And I know that when the Tall Trees harvest begins, I will leave for a vacation.

Today there's a different harvest in the forest.

As I wander down the trail into the shadowy trees, I surprise four brush pickers. They're crouched beside the path in chest-high undergrowth, harvesting salal sprigs for local floral companies for national distribution.

"Ola" I greet them and smile. Why not be friendly?

They stare at me, and I them. They don't say a word. Mutual distrust and danger instantly arise to overshadow the moment. The men are like animals caught with no escape route. They coil back while considering their next move. Suddenly, I'm unsure what my next step should be.

Not all tales these woods can tell are good. Two years ago, half-a-mile from here, rival brush pickers traded gunfire in a territorial harvesting rights dispute. Others recently pointed a gun at a teenager and demanded access to private property to pick brush. I am carrying an expensive camera. Since the shooting incident, many forest supervisors who monitor picking boundaries have given up trying to regulate harvesting rights. Most floral companies lease land where they send pickers, but some companies buy from whoever shows up with a truckload of greenery and don't ask questions. Undergrowth disappears from the forest. And often from private property.

Last fall, while hunting for chanterelles in thick underbrush in a nearby forest, I stepped on a plastic bag with something inside. I kicked the bag. A bloody knife blade slid through the plastic. The knife was not a fishing knife. Shocked, I rushed away and didn't pick it up. I thought of returning to find the grisly knife to hand over to the police, but by the time I decided to go back, knew it would be impossible to retrace my steps through the dense undergrowth and I didn't want to stay another moment in such a spooky place.

I keep walking along Tall Trees Trail, but after a short distance turn around, feeling it in my best interest to leave the forest to the brush pickers. As I approach them again, one of them stares at me and asks in broken English:

"Ees OK?"

"It's State land. I don't know the rules. You should know them."

One of the others further down the trail eyes me warily as I add, "Please don't pick ALL the undergrowth!"

"Thank you." He nods his head, grins, relieved that I appear friendly, and goes back to picking as I walk away. I, too, feel somewhat relieved.

I don't think any of them has understood a word I said.

The men work in constant fear of being caught and deported to countries that offer poverty and sometimes worse. Weekly, pickers line up at the local convenience store to wire money to families in Mexico and Guatemala. I hope that someday these men can live without fear and with security for their families. I also hope that they do not totally strip the forest of undergrowth. At the same time, I know that before long the whole forest will be gone.

I return to our five acres, saddened once more by stories stirred while hiking trails so close to home.

☼

Grateful for the privacy and safety of our land, I detour through a stand of trees by the river trailhead brushing through conifers that blend in a medley of sap scent and healing green aura, each conifer with its distinctive leaves or needles: long slender pine needles, short stubby fir, shiny irregular hemlock needles and lacy cedar fronds. Vine maple fill gaps between the conifers with leaves that droop like half-opened lime-green umbrellas from a web of red twigs.

A woodpecker's jackhammer beak pounds like heavy artillery, his Herculean neck muscles working long hours, as he drills for ant hors d'oeuvres and insect entrees.

Last week's white trilliums have turned pink, lilac and maroon. Curled shepherd's-crook stems of young sword ferns unfurl like a circle of bent-over dancers unrolling their spines upward. By the riverbank, smaller bracken wave tentative feathery arms. A loud bumblebee dances rings around me three times then takes off after warning me that this is his grubstake.

Earlier this spring I watched a tiny shoot struggle into life between grains of sand in a crevice of a weatherworn trunk in the logjam. Now the shoot is ten inches high and I recognize the crinkled leaves of a baby alder. Resilient nature grabs hold in even the most adverse conditions. And alder seeds sprout easily. If only conifers in clear-cuts could grow as fast, but then they'd be harvested as fast too.

Late April stamps like an impatient colt. I watch my own impatience. Each day I return to the same plants, wait and watch for a baby leaf or first blossom. I covet a photo of the exquisite opening of a flower or leaf but often nature has rushed ahead. The leaf is open and flowers bloom, but an army of insects has munched holes in the leaf and crawl over pretty petals with no respect for my aesthetic ideal. From a mossy bank, a clump of false Solomon seal shoots up veined leaves, but the foliage dematerializes fast and the race is on between plant and insect. Insects are gaining ground. Too bad I'm not an insect photographer.

I would be very pleased with a photo of a luminous shaft of sunlight in an April glade but days and days of wind and rain deny a luminous shaft of sunlight, and instead of a fairytale glade, a haphazard mess of tangled fractured branches, broken ferns and uprooted trees reveal the true underworld face of the forest.

I learn to appreciate the perfection of chaos and dissolution; I learn to applaud nature in disarray; I learn to let go of expectations and manmade concepts of beauty; and I learn to value shadows and darkness. The underlying ragged beauty of nature is always far more intricate and complex and 'right' than either the human eye can perceive or the judgmental conditioned mind comprehend.

A silver sky blends with the gray of the pebble beach and weathered logjam. Although the river flows fast after last week's rain, ambient tranquility of the water lulls me with its rippling pulse. For a magic instant a pale sun slices through the gray and flashes light across small rapids. A chorus of birdsong blends in concert with an aria of river water. A hummingbird, first of the season, zooms past with a shrill 'shreeem' on his way to suck salmonberry nectar.

Crouching close to the water's edge I scan the water for baby fish. First one tiny finned wiggler, then another, catches my attention and once my eyes are accustomed to their underwater darting, I count a dozen baby salmon. The salmonids, two inches long, iridescent light gray with pinkish tail fins, face upstream in the shallows, take in water and oxygen through open mouths then release it through their gills. Although they appear to be trying to swim upstream against the fast current, they're just waiting, feeding on whatever comes their way. For the first months of life they idle in holding areas and gorge on bugs before swimming downstream to the ocean. Then, three years from now, they'll be back.

More baby salmon dart to attention in a deep pond by the logjam. A bug brushes the water's surface and zwup, no more bug. I tease half-a-dozen salmonids from shadowy hideouts by tossing pieces of alder catkin. They zip and squiggle to the potential treat, but realizing my trick, the little fish soon relax back to lazy shallows paddling.

I'm happy by the river. Before long, I'll be a summer native of the river valley. I'll sun bathe on the beach, skinny-dip and shallows paddle alongside the baby salmon.

CHAPTER 6

CRESCENDO OF BUZZ

PETALS FLUTTER from cherry trees in the orchard. Bees sample nectar. Camera-ready, I wait under flowering branches for the perfect photo of a perfect bee on a perfect cherry blossom. I shoot bees landing on flowers, quickly sipping nectar and flitting over petals, but when I examine the shots later, where are the bees? My mind, eye, hand and camera are too slow to capture the fleeting instant the bees pause at each flower. Cherry blossom produces little useable nectar, chosen by bees only if there's no alternative, and the bees don't linger. Today other irresistible sources capture their attention– chartreuse maple tassels.

Leaving the orchard to check the 'kitchen beehive', so named because I can watch its residents from the window above the kitchen sink, I notice another alternative, a stack of old beehive frames smeared with traces of last year's honey. Although we started the kitchen hive just two days ago, the bees are already well established. Bee droppings, small round yellow dots, splotch the hive top and ground in front of the entrance. Bees, hygienic creatures, won't foul travel boxes and will wait to fly outside for a bathroom break. So far, washing hung on the clothesline by the kitchen hasn't been targeted, but before long, work-wear will be T-shirts and jeans speckled with yellow dots.

Inside the hive, the queen, who can produce as many as an amazing two thousand eggs a day (and a million from a single mating), has begun to lay eggs in the waxy frame cells. But a handful of workers still wander aimlessly inside the small queen cage, enamored by her lingering scent. I shoo them out into the hive and remove the cage.

When bee birthrate outstrips available nectar, and with dubious weather for nectar hunting, we must sometimes supplement feed for the new hives. A day or two of rain will keep bees inside and soon deplete reserve honey stores. As a precaution I set a Ziploc bag of sugar-water, with holes poked through the top, on top of the frames. If the weather is good and flowers bloom nearby, the bees will choose flower nectar over the sugar syrup any day.

Our bee yard at Beards Cove, where we over-winter most of our hives, huddles in a protected corner of an old homestead deserted for many years. The land is now protected Hood Canal wetlands. Only a small pile of rubble remains of the forgotten homestead, but the legacy of a cultivated garden remains. Trees and shrubs planted years ago by settlers have re-seeded and spread to entwine with a wild sprawl of brambles, high marsh grass and alder. Domestic flowers have naturalized to the wild, clumps of bluebells brighten a brushy thicket, last year's unharvested figs hang from a gnarled fig tree, and buds on an overgrown lilac bulge with future fragrance. Last winter, a weeping willow, long past middle age but not quite ancient, lost a third of the tree when soft wood of the trunk split and fell during a storm; young branches still shower layers of swaying green curtains from the fallen third for one last year. Fortunately the falling limbs missed our hives. By inches.

Sunbeams dance lace shadows through a leaf ceiling of flowering salmonberry above the path from the highway to the bee yard. Lilac-colored herb Robert, whisks of horsetail, white starflowers, nettle and dandelion nestle in thick grass at my feet.

Sunshine warms the air to sixty-five degrees. Thousands of field bees are out flying to replenish their larder, with meal choices changing daily as bud after bud opens to pour out nectar and pollen. Days like these are best to work inside the hives, with fewer field bees at home to be disturbed by large nosy white-clad animals.

The air vibrates with the zip and zing of golden girls loaded with pollen and nectar. In France, beekeepers call bees '*fils du soleil*', 'daughters of the sun'. I know why. As the bees circle and hover above the hives, they glow, glint and flash yellow dots like miniature suns spinning through the universe. Roy calls his bees 'the girls'.

In a yard of seventy colonies, with millions of bees, I'm constantly amazed how each bee knows her way home. But then again, when I think of how millions of people maneuver through their daily work routine in Boston or Tokyo and return home safely to the suburbs at night, I'm even more amazed. The homing instinct is intuitively natural for all species. A bee uses her queen's scent pheromones as a homing device, and we use memory. But underlying that memory, perhaps we too rely on an ancient instinctive sense of smell no longer in the forefront of consciousness. We have all experienced the pleasant feeling of 'Yes! I'm home,' as we step into the familiar scent of where we live.

Bees from new hives fly alongside bees from older hives. I remove handfuls of dead grass previously stuffed in entry openings of the new hives to deter robber bees. Young hives with few bees need the extra protection of a small entrance until the hives are sufficiently populated to guard their threshold.

We take apart the over-wintered hives, even as field bees stash the latest honey delivery inside the frames and newly hatched girls busily housekeep and tend to larvae nursing duties. One by one we gently take off the boxes and set them on the ground to access the bottom board for cleaning. I scrape away debris from screen boards (metal screens attached to the bottom board).

The screen boards are one way we deter parasitic varroa mites. When mites fall off the bees, they drop through the screens and cannot climb back up again. Roy approaches the mite problem from several angles, constantly searching for holistic solutions to this scourge of bee loss. Russian queens, whose offspring have the reputation of hygienic behavior, are another line of defense. The varroa epidemic has decimated apiaries worldwide and hundreds of beekeepers have quit the beekeeping business.

In winter, bees begin by eating honey stored in the bottom box, feeding from side to side, and then slowly move up. Now the bottom box is empty, and in the second box, the brood box, the queen scurries around laying eggs. Workers cap brood cells. Larvae hatch. We switch bottom boxes with top boxes. By switching boxes the bees will again have space to work upward.

Inside stronger hives, masses of bees swirl like a sea in constant motion. Workers line up and hover at the entrance for a turn to deliver their goods. Evenly spaced velvety brood patterns cover frames where the queen has laid an egg in every cell. And several boxes are already heavy with fresh honey.

But at the back of the bee yard, three or four hives have not fared as well. When I lift one lid, dead bees litter the top of the frames. Ants have overtaken the distressed hive and crawl over honey left in the cells. In another, a mouse has built a nest in the lower box after munching through the wax foundation. A hive can spiral downhill fast. Even if there is still an egg-laying queen there may be too few workers to nurse larvae, gather nectar and pollen, and defend the hive. And there must be enough bees to maintain a hive temperature necessary for survival.

Disease, mites, pesticide and starvation are the main causes of bee loss. In two of the dead hives there are no outward signs of disease or mites and we suspect that the bees succumbed to pesticide poisoning. Even though people believe they spray their garden or the highway shoulder 'safely', tiny quantities of toxic residue can kill or severely weaken bees who ingest the poison or pick up particles on their hair. Organo-phosphates, which attack the insect's nervous system, are the worst.

One of the keys to a healthy hive is a strong queen, and some of last year's colonies are amazing. Our resilient Russian queens work non-stop to fill frame after frame with brood, soon to hatch into vigorous young bees. We add boxes to the hives. Some hive skyscrapers already tower five boxes high: two deep boxes at the bottom and three shallow honey supers on top. If the good weather holds, we will have a record honey year. As long as no one sprays nearby.

While I work inside the hives, everything outside disappears. Perhaps the intoxicating sweetness has something to do with it. The pace is slow/fast, the trancelike speed of intensity, clarity and increased awareness. Intruding on the bees' privacy, I attempt to practice gentleness, disturbing the bees as little as possible, but I'm large and clumsy compared to the small agile insects. When rearranging the environment inside a hive we often cause distress and upset a number of sensitive bees. Understandable, when the bees arrive home loaded with supplies and find their home completely dismantled or significantly altered, while big, gloved hands with metal hive tools poke around inside.

The temperature inside my bee suit rises like a New York elevator without air-conditioning on an August day. The usual steady mellow hum of the yard crescendos with the escalating buzz of disturbed bees as bees crawl over every inch of my protective clothing and veil. Once one hive becomes upset, other hives smell the spreading alarm pheromones and join them in preparing for an emergency. A handful of guard bees bombard me with a hot and angry repeat of "BUZZ OFF! GO AWAY!" Then, within minutes, hundreds of relentless insects fling their bodies against the thin netting of my veil, making as intense a mega-decibel sound as bees can make (equaled only by surround-sound of a bee horror movie). Which of course is amplified by my rising emotion. The bees smell the scent of my anxiety and know they're getting to me with their frenzied attack. It takes all my courage and stamina to continue.

The bees win. Overcome by the intensity, I drop my hive tool, walk out of the yard and escape to the shade of a nearby fir. Guards follow, aggressive warnings buzzing loud around me. I stand still and relax until they slowly lose interest and one by one fly back to the hives. My ears ring in the silence.

Out of the newfound quiet, gentler sounds of a mellow spring day soothe my ringing ears. The sweetness of birdsong brings harmony back into my world, the distant swoosh of cars echoes along a highway and a light breeze blows cool and refreshing through my veil. From high above, small fir cones release a fine dust of yellow pollen into the spring air.

☼

The next bee yard has fewer colonies. The site, again left to return to the wild, was once a meadow, a ploughed field and a small orchard. Old pear trees in full bloom circle the yard. The grown-wild trees stretch toward an azure sky with a froth of white flowers, while smaller re-seeded trees, under the giants, shower confetti of snowflake petals onto the hives. We work under blossoming branches of one weathered pear tree that towers more than sixty feet overhead.

Bramble forests wrestle for supremacy over the land. Blackberry rules. Feisty vines stretch up, then arch downward with a ten-foot spiny reach. If left alone, nature will reclaim this land, not with its original face, but with a challenging beauty heralded by invasive tough plant and animal species brought to the region by man.

As expected, bees thrive in the circle of blossom, but, as at the previous yard, some hives have succumbed to death by possible pesticide.

High in the branches of a tall fir across the road from the bee yard, a proud white head watches over the countryside from the broad rim of the eagle's nest. Too bad the eagle can't warn bees, or humans, of the dangers of pesticides–although not many years ago, rapid decline of eagle populations to near extinction, attributed to DDT, did just that.

☼

Chapter 7

NEW NEICHBORS

A GARTER SNAKE, black with yellow stripes, basks in weak sunshine at the river trailhead. Curled snugly in a pile of dead leaves, he eyes me warily but doesn't shift an inch as I edge closer to admire his sinuous curves.

When I first moved here, excessive snakes gliding through undergrowth triggered fear. I would jump when I saw one–or two. Fear was understandable. At different times in my life I've lived in serious snake-country West Africa, India and Southwest US desert. Now, I rarely startle, knowing that no poisonous snakes live west of the Cascades, and instead, their flowing movement, absolute stillness and darting tongues are a welcome fascination. Plus I learned that they eat slugs. Snakes in a garden are a good thing.

Another garter snake crosses my path. He freezes mid-wiggle. A tangerine stripe lines the center of his back with pale lemon stripes on either side. After countless seconds of stopped time, the slitherer eases under cover of dead leaves in controlled slow motion. So many snakes must be a good omen. Although a surprising flicker of unidentifiable subconscious memory, danger, or premonition crosses my mind.

The woodlands vibrate with birdsong. I don't try to identify the intricate variety of calls and melodies of birds rejoicing their return to summer temperate forests but stand still and let the concert of unnamed warblers soak into me. I absorb ascending and descending runs, chirps, repeated trills, dweep-dweeps, chickerings, whistles and peeps.

Do we lose the mystery and spontaneous joy of unnamed experience when we label and examine too closely? Appreciation at a holistic level beyond words allows an intimacy between the consciousness of the 'act' and the 'acted upon', a union where everything vanishes except the thrilling experience of the essence of the sound. Just as the eye of a camera captures less than one second of a scene, recording it forever in a limited way, naming of birds in the woods may lessen and cut short the experience of a forest alive with a symphony of birdsong. Whenever I am tempted at the first recognized birdcall to say 'ah yes, that's a...,' I remember to listen at a deeper level to the nuance, changes, individuality and soul of each song, as well as the overall kaleidoscope of sound. Perhaps only poetry can truly reflect ecstatic heart melodies sung by feathered friends as they rustle and swoop through young leaves of early spring.

Halfway down the river trail I pause beside a group of eye-catching crumpled false morels that push through dead leaves at my feet. Engrossed in the magical world of mulch and mushroom, I reach for my camera, crouch, then kneel and sink my chin to the damp leaf mold to line up an eye level shot.

A snapped branch cracks like gunfire from across a steep gully to my right. I freeze. Voices echo. Still kneeling, my awareness sharpens instantly as if hit by a Zen stick. I scan the hillside through disheveled leafing trees. Two men are headed downhill a hundred yards away. Heavy footsteps crunch through the underbrush and mossy forest deadfall.

My heart lurches.

Who are these men? Are they brush-pickers? Why are they here?

They haven't seen me. I'll surprise them. Hunched low, with the stealth of a coyote, I scurry as quietly as I can down the trail to reach the valley floor before them. As they hike closer, I strain to hear their words.

"Wow. Great place for picnic tables."

"Yeah. Great place."

In MY woods! Picnic tables!

They're talking about the wild place of swampy ponds, domain of eerie mystery and shadows where branches tangle in savage beauty and shiny skunk cabbage grow in big leaf profusion: my primitive haven full of nests, holes and webs, breeding place and home to masses of frogs and insects.

My brain switches to overdrive. My whole perspective shifts as my pleasant afternoon exploration takes on an unexpected bitter flavor of "NO! I don't want these people here!"

The five-acre parcel of land on the south side of our property has been for sale for more than a year. We'd like to buy the land to store beehives and ensure our privacy, but the price is high and we don't have the funds. Maybe the men are prospective buyers.

I reach the valley floor, hurry along the trail parallel to the river then cautiously approach the men. They see me; they hesitate, startled, then keep walking toward me. I draw myself up, block the path and confront them with a sharp "Hi". I startle myself. My usual style is not to assert myself in the woods. My woodland mode is more along the lines of 'melt into the leaves'.

Trying to hide the quaver in my voice I demand: "Are you buying the property? Are you going to be our neighbors?"

"...workin' on agreement with th'owners," mumbles one of the men. The other shifts his weight from foot to foot and looks around, not interested in holding a conversation with an unexpected woman in the woods. Neither wants to meet my eye. They're slouchy, slightly unkempt, in their thirties. The mumbler wears bib overalls over a plaid flannel shirt. The jittery one, a redhead in a red t-shirt, looks like he can't wait to move away.

The mumbler and I garble a brief conversation about the property line. The redhead points to a pink plastic ribbon tied to an alder and draws an imaginary line in the air directly from the marker to the river, which includes—on their side—the path to the river beach and the beach itself.

The river beach on the neighbor's property! How is that possible? Only a small piece of cut-away riverbank would be on our land. I take a moment to digest the unexpected and extremely unwelcome information.

As I pause to understand the unnerving situation, they brush past me and march down the path to the beach as if they already own it. They claim the pebbled river shore, victorious. I don't follow them.

"Hey, this is awesome!" the jittery one shouts.

Invaders. I'm in shock. In three years, I haven't seen anyone in the woods. No neighbors live to the north, and dense State Forest stretches for miles on the far side of the river. Within moments the heavy boots, loud voices and roughness of these men have violated my whispering backwater refuge. I'm shaking.

Attempting to regain composure, I retreat upstream and collapse onto a weathered log, surprised by how upset I feel. Tears roll down my cheeks. Without warning, some of my sacred hideaways will no long be mine for private wandering and contemplation. What will the newcomers do with the land? Will they build picnic tables and throw loud parties? And with no beach, where will I sit, meditate, and lose myself to the murmur of the river? And where will I swim naked?

How easily I thought I owned the place. I forget I am also an intruder on nature and how my own insensitivity and noise must horrify native animals and plants. Not to mention how bees must feel when I invade their hives.

I remember to breathe, slow down, and remind myself that letting go and change are the natural flow of life, even if preceded by pain. Letting go of my privacy is difficult, but letting go of my attachment to a wilderness that might soon be radically changed is far more difficult. I am faced with the extent of my unconscious grasping, holding and owning as I harbor selfish desires for wild ways of my private forest sanctuary to thrive forever, and want everything to conform to MY private worldview.

The knife of sudden sadness cuts open my narrow perspective. I wipe my tear-streaked face with the back of my hand and try bravely to struggle beyond my limited thinking.

As if feeling my sorrow, a frog plops into the river beside my log perch. My connection to nature, shrunk in contraction from the shock of the encounter, opens into a deeper, more profound connection with the appearance of this untamed creature of the forest. Frog arrives at exactly the right moment.

Frog, the animal totem for emotion, eases the passage for tears of release. Frog, master of transformation and metamorphosis, amphibian living both on land and underwater, melts and heals with cleansing wetness. Frog, bringer of showers, floods, singer of the ways of weather, signals that change is on the way.

Perhaps the newcomers will learn to treasure wildness. Perhaps the newcomers will raise children who grow wise from hours exploring the riverbanks. Perhaps the newcomers will learn quiet reverence for nature. Perhaps the newcomers will move away. Soon.

Heavy and confused, I leave the valley floor to the invaders and climb back up the river trail. I share the disturbing news with Roy. He's shocked. We immediately hike back to the river to check exactly where the property line falls. The men are gone. We dig into the mossy leaf-mold and uncover plastic markers. The markers indicate that the property line doesn't run straight to the river as the redhead thought, but cuts diagonally through woods south of both the path and the beach.

Yes! The beach is not lost to us.

But how will we get along with the new neighbors?

Chapter 8

MAY WINDS

A ROWDY WIND sways treetops and cleans stale air from the clearing. Old dead limbs, weak branches and brittle twigs hurtle to the ground. Fir pollen dusts a veil of lemon powder on every surface. Wind dissolves the old, pollinates the new, blows cool and fierce to strengthen infant shoots. Wind tests plants before unexpected trials of summer.

Vulnerable and shaky from yesterday's encounter with the potential neighbors, I struggle to keep my mind from imagining what they might do to our wild environment. Inevitable changes, like the slow growth of a tree and natural shifts of a child's journey into adulthood are acceptable, whereas sudden unanticipated change is far less palatable.

The woods and river have been my safe harbor and refuge. Our property will continue to be my safe haven and refuge. And even if the neighbors cut all the trees on their land and throw wild parties, the river will not disappear and acres and acres of surrounding forest still survive.

So why am I afraid?

A deer appears in the orchard to interrupt my uneasy thoughts. She grazes between the cherry trees, nibbles and munches from juicy tuft to juicy tuft of emerald green, flicks an ear at a passing fly every now and then, lifts her head, glances around and listens, always chewing on her simple meal. For half-an-hour the deer inches through the orchard, relaxed and unconcerned, then steps away lightly up the driveway. She softens and quiets my distress. Perhaps I am overly anxious about our new neighbors.

Despite the gray and windy weather for the first day of May, plus my recent unpleasant encounter, I feel bright when I think of ancient Britain's May Day maypole dances, celebrations of laughter and carefree sharing of sensual pleasure. To honor old traditions I gather branches from nine flowering trees and shrubs to decorate inside our home. I pick pear, apple, cherry, cascara, Oregon grape, red currant, plum, willow and salmonberry branches, all loaded with blossom. I harvest fragrant herbs–sage, thyme, oregano and rosemary–and tie them in a bundle with shiny satin ribbons.

I light a candle made with sweet-smelling beeswax from our hives. The flame dips and flickers as I envision the sacred bonfires of Beltane when fires from nine types of tree blazed on hilltops all across the English countryside. Visible for miles and miles, these fires, beacons of hope and celebration, joined villages across the land as each community performed elaborate ceremonies. Beltane was also the Celtic day of prayers offered to the Gods for the protection of flocks and herds. To honor the tradition I invoke a short prayer for the well being of our bees in their perilous work of honey gathering at the beginning of the twenty-first century.

A shipment of new queen bees has arrived at the Tahuya post office. We drive nine winding miles through undeveloped woods and forest down to the Hood Canal where the post office nestles near the mouth of the Tahuya River.

A trailing groundcover of pink-flowered kinnikinnick blankets roadside slopes. Bell-shaped flowers of shiny-leaved huckleberry hover above the sprawling kinnikinnick. Light pink huckleberry flowers bloom first at the top of reddish stems then open down the stems for an extra long nectar flow, a plus for our bees. Not every year is fruitful, but this year masses of buds load the branches, promising a bumper crop of flowers and berries. Above the huckleberry bushes, taller scrubby stands of pink-blossomed manzanita crown the blooming trio. The evergreen family look like mama, papa and baby, each clasping pale pink bouquets.

Alongside the trio of soft pinks, garish yellow flowers of Scotch broom light every roadside ditch and bank. Broom infests the Pacific Northwest with splashy golden rain that overpowers weaker native flora, and with minimal requirements for fertile soil, the scrubby invasive plant spreads like wildfire. Any old dirt will do. If nature is a race for survival of the fittest, then scotch broom jostles right up there with the winners.

Behind the scrubby bushes on either side of the highway rise acres and acres of fir. Some trees were planted as recently as two years ago, some five, ten or twenty years ago. But more hillsides are clear-cut than grown up. The timber industry harvests younger and younger trees. Logging trucks, once weighed down by three or four giant logs, now race to mills with spindly matchsticks. Wood chip and sawdust products replace lumber as the large trees vanish.

The steep hill to the Canal winds through a vaulted cathedral of evergreen arches and newly leafed deciduous branches. My mind jumps quickly from the sad disappearance of big trees to the beauty of creamy dogwood blossoms floating on the strong breeze like slow butterflies above a green sea.

The road follows the Tahuya River to its tidal mouth where wind gusts ruffle high tide water lapping against the Tahuya Bridge. Canadian geese bob on the disheveled estuary. Banks of tideland sedges swish and ripple in silken waves.

A sudden ferocious gust roars through swaying treetops. The gust whips and swirls across the open wetlands, licks river water into a frenzy and bends low any growing thing. Only flexible young trees and supple plants with strong roots can survive this driven force of wind. Older trees–brittle willow, soft cottonwood, rotting maple and alder–split, topple and slough off rigid limbs. The gust reminds me to examine and slough off my own rigid attitudes.

Stacked boxes of queens await us at the post office. The grinning postmaster and other postal workers question us, curious about the strange medley of high-pitched peeps echoing from the packages. This is by far the most fascinating delivery of the day. We pick up the packages but will wait to hive the queens. The wind is too cold and fierce to risk opening hive lids.

At home, wind shimmies through the clearing in a rush of green, building intensity till the rustling sway of leaves drowns all sounds of the river. Another trial by wind for baby leaves. Is this an omen for summer tests that await us too?

Drifts of white sweet-smelling wood-smoke float from giant smoldering stump piles half a mile to the south where a new road is being built. A dirt road becomes an asphalt highway and the road to the forest becomes the road through the forest.

Refusing to allow thoughts of the recent intrusion to deter me, I hike to the river. Above the river path lacy chartreuse maple leaves and deep-veined alder leaves dance a swirling green collage. Everywhere on the forest floor, small clenched fern fists unfold skyward. Last week, toothy sword fern fronds stood six inches to a foot. Now they measure one to two feet with new sabers that unfurl as if the brownish green spirals will reach upward forever. Perhaps they'll form an impenetrable wall of green to protect from unwanted neighbors.

I pull a piece of licorice fern from a mossy trunk and chew on the root. The root, which Indians chewed as a sweetener and cough medicine, has a light licorice flavor. Next to a side stream, fragile maidenhair spreads luminous leaves from straight dark stems. Pale new bracken fronds–the world's most widespread fern–shoot from the shallow riverbank. Brackens' all-powerful roots reach deep to survive forest fires. The determined plant thrusts through thick underbrush and bursts without warning from scanty-soiled cracks and crevices. Not always where welcome.

The woodlands sway with every shape and texture and every shade of green from palest lime to brilliant emerald to dark evergreen. Tiny white, pink and purple buds and flowers splatter the moving canvas. By the creek, tight river reeds wave fuzzy brown heads. On other reeds that look like African spears, tangled white hair flies from tough green shafts topped by sleek black spikes.

I explore the riverbank in woods north of our property, away from thoughts of neighbors and closer to a friendlier environment of beaver dams and the beavers' main lodge. Steep mud skids angle into the river every hundred feet. Piles of newly chewed small trees clutter slopes where clearing and dragging are the order of the day for a major construction project. Beaver can alter an environment faster than any animal other than humans, but at least they don't add picnic tables to natural hidden places.

Small green and red plants sprout from sand between pebbles. Tentacle-like roots criss-cross stones, reaching into every crevice to scrounge succor for young spikes and shoots. In a muddy creek bed off the main river, yellow skunk cabbage sheaths have faded and wilted, exposing flower stems where swarms of black bugs suck the last juice from dull greenish blossoms.

Memories of my encounter with the new neighbors fade.

On a bush close to the beach, creamy ironwood flowers froth like white lilacs. Indians used the hard wood from the ironwood tree, also known as oceanspray creambush, for spears, digging sticks, harpoon shafts and pegs.

Sudden screeches ring from the other side of the river. The distressed cries echo through the woods again and again, but I cannot identify what animal makes a sound halfway between the bark of a small dog and a short human scream. Perhaps a large rodent. A crow, the most inquisitive bird around, arrives to investigate the screams from a nearby treetop but leaves as soon as the cries quiet. Someone with whom he is not interested in competing has obviously grabbed his chance at a meal. The sound of the wind settles once more through the woods.

Beaver have chewed through another copse of young maples leaving chunk-tooth autographed stumps. In an ecological race, an endless supply of saplings rushes to revitalize pruned riverbanks with shoots to appease the beavers' appetite and building requirements. The beavers have left me a beautiful walking stick, a straight five-foot-long staff, peeled and whittled white.

The windswept day also gifts me color, texture and design: a Stellar's jay feather; a two-inch-round gray paper wasp nest fallen on the path, shell and inner parchment layers all intact; the sight of an orange ladybug under lime green leaves in a crook of scarlet vine maple twigs and a slinky black and lemon garter snake wind-sheltered by a smooth white marble rock.

CHAPTER 9

THE GARDEN

LYING FLAT on my back on the clover, grass, moss and dandelion lawn, I close my eyes, melt like butter into the earth and dissolve in the sensual sound and sunshine of late spring. Bumblebees drone from dandelion to dandelion: buzz, then silence, buzz, and then silence. Above, the flutter of bird wings and songs of the wind brushing through needled tree boughs. Opening my eyes to puffy cloud billows I watch seven swallows loop and swoop, dive and weave through bent tips of sixty-foot hemlocks at the lawn's edge on their yearly return to nest under woodshed eaves.

A mowing machine grinds down a county road in the distance, and I'm grateful that local officials have chosen this alternative to spraying. Two weeks after the sweep of a mower the grass re-grows and ditch-water remains unpolluted.

The all-around kinetic busyness of springtime teases me to leave my earthy bed and visit the wilderness of the unkempt garden. Half-a-dozen crops survive from last year. I salvage a salad of chickweed, dandelion greens, peppergrass, parsley, chives and broccoli-like shoots from kale going to flower and complete the salad with a sprinkling of purple and yellow pansy petals.

51

Along the far edge of the garden, supple leafy raspberry canes lazily stretch out and arch over like rose bowers. Buds are taut with bloom. Rhubarb expands at a fantastic rate, fertilized both by the compost pile and a potent organic mess left from cleaning beehive bottom boards. Outside the garden fence, next to the chicken coop, horseradish fed by seepage of old chicken manure shoots up with explosive growth.

The chicken coop is deserted. Last winter all our small flock of two old bad-tempered Rhode Island Reds and seven young shiny black Austerlops died. On a stormy night, when heavy rain drowned all sound, a weasel crept into the coop and murdered every one. We didn't hear a thing, and neither did Zap, who usually barks at the slightest unusual sound.

Eerie silence surrounded the coop when I went to let the chickens out in the morning. A crumpled chicken sprawled against the wire mesh. Trails of blood and feathers led the way to all the other birds who had tried to hide under the roost and nesting boxes. Several months before, rats had snuck into the chicken house to steel feed, leaving small holes at ground level in the chicken wire. I hadn't paid attention, not overly concerned by the rats' petty theft. What a mistake.

The weasel didn't even eat any of the chickens. When the weasel tried to drag a chicken victim through a small opening in the wire fence, the chicken's body lodged in the too-small hole. If a wily coyote occasionally took a chicken, I didn't mind, but this was a senseless act of innocent chicken slaughter. I mourned the sudden loss of my feathered friends and decided not to keep more chickens this year. I still miss them.

Roy fires up the rototiller and takes on the garden. Not an easy task with the unwieldy lumbering machine, but a huge improvement over tackling the heavy muddy chore of digging the expanse with a shovel. The rototiller quickly turns under a thick blanket of winter clover and all other weedy cover crops, and by late afternoon the garden is hilled up with rows of raised beds ready to plant.

Last year I saved vegetable seeds to plant this year. And in February I ordered extra seeds through the mail, a time of year I yearly succumb to seduction by the deluge of garden catalogs. I ogle page after page of over-saturated color and poetic descriptions while my imagination flies to bumper crops of unblemished super vegetables and an ecstatic orgy of flowers. Dreaming of summer-bright gaudy blossoms–the gaudier the better–with heady eye-closing fragrance and, of course, thousands of bees, exaggerated expectations nowhere play themselves out as dramatically as my gardening thoughts in late winter. While delicate woodland wildflowers touch my heart, and speak to me in tender, gentle ways, I'm also a pushover for the sumptuous splash and swagger of blossoms enhanced by human ingenuity, glorified and made famous in every garden catalog and magazine.

This year I'll plant red and orange flowers for ever more flash. Calendula, California poppies, red crest cosmos, butterfly weed and orange amaranth. The garden already blazes with red azaleas, red rhodies, red dahlias, crimson bee balm and sprawling clusters of scarlet poppies. Dandelion, vetch, yarrow and Shasta daisies bloom white, purple and yellow all summer long in high orchard grass. Pink penstemon, lupines, ajuga, sweet william, valerian, fuchsia-colored yarrow, lavender, blue delphiniums and flowering herbs spread soft pinks, blues and purples through the yard. I'll expand the palette with rainbow chard and Japanese ornamental maize with pink, white, yellow and green striped leaves, dark purple tassels and maroon kernels. The garden will be a visual riot. And attract pollinators.

After dinner I place six kinds of beans in jars to soak overnight: Scarlet runners, Oceana's summer, New Hampshire horticultural, and two kinds saved from last year whose names are long forgotten, plus one type of bean Roy calls Grandma's beans. For years he searched for beans similar to those brought by his grandmother from Yugoslavia half a century ago and finally found some last year in an old canning jar in a thrift store. But will they germinate?

☼

The new Moon emerges from her dark cycle. Planting time.

A visiting friend, Shanti, a singer of classical East Indian chants, joins us in a ceremony to honor the earth and to pray for blessings for a successful growing season and plentiful harvest.

I spread a map of the world on the ground and place a generous vase of blossoms at its center. We pile packets of vegetable and flower seeds around the base.

We pray:

> that our planting will be a symbolic act for nurturing the world and an end to hunger;
> that people in every country will have access to, can use and save good seeds;
> that people everywhere will have the opportunity to grow nourishing food for themselves and their families if they choose;
> that the earth's depleted soil is replenished and made healthy;
> that corporate industry won't destroy the balance of nature more than it already has with pesticides, herbicides, seed monopolies, biotech experiments and genetic engineering;
> that plants and animals thrive in natural environments;
> that humans have the sense to work in harmony with nature for restoration and the honoring of biodiversity;
> that these seeds will grow into strong wholesome plants giving us health, nourishment and beauty.

We thank the earth for providing us the seeds.

We sing, chant and shake bean jar rattles under falling cherry, plum and apple blossom petals.

I mix all the annual flower seeds together in one cup. No size or color discrimination here. The flowers will germinate and grow wherever they fall to surprise me with spontaneous beauty. Or random chaos. The Jackson Pollock approach to planting.

At the newly prepared flowerbed along the workshop wall Shanti and I chant, scatter seeds and brush them with a light layer of soil. A row of Japanese ornamental maize earns special placement. Seeds of future color slip through our fingers into fresh brown dirt beds around the lawn as we sing and chant to Gods and Goddesses of the harvest.

In the vegetable garden, after cultivating rich dark earth in raised beds to prepare them for planting, we rake and mark rows and create small pathways for sprinkler access. Two rows of seven-foot-high beanpoles already create a trellis parallel to the garden's back fence. Chanting again, we plant the bean seeds around the poles, then turn to the raised beds and plant two types of carrots, parsnip, rainbow chard, beets, three types of kale, salad mix, amaranth, radish and two types of peas, all while holding awareness and reverence for the miracle of transformation of seeds to full-grown plants.

When we first began planting, there was far more space than would ever be needed, with a projected harvest of enough to feed five families. Now I wonder where we'll plant zucchini, several kinds of squash and tomatoes. Plus a row of flowers. Every Valentine's day I give Roy and his son, Ian, a packet of flower seeds so that Valentine's flowers will be enjoyed all summer long.

With gentle rain falling now, Shanti and I leave the garden and walk up the driveway scattering flower seeds I collected last year–columbine, lupine, anise hyssop and scarlet campion–in scrubby dirt on either side of the road. Ominous clouds loom overhead but hold to a soft sprinkle until we sow the last seed. Then rain shifts gears to soak and swell the seeds, perfectly timed to bring to life the future garden of color, scent and taste already blossoming in my imagination.

☼

Rain showers have varnished grass blades pearly-wet and shiny.

After a week of impatient waiting, I check to see if seeds have germinated. Yes! First tiny leaves of radish, kale, carrot, lettuce and amaranth poke through crumbly earth on top of the raised beds. As well as upstart grass and chickweed hustling a free drink of sprinkler rain. Young bright grass crowds the garden perimeter, elbowing in on the rich dark soil. The lush barrier of perimeter grass provides a comfortable environment for hungry bugs and insects (though around here they're seldom hungry). Healthy well-fed bugs are less prone to explode into plague-like swarms for survival of their species. And hiding silently in the tall grass, many a tongue-darting snake awaits a good bug meal.

A patch of hearty shoots pushes through soil where I planted Swiss chard, and I know they are not chard. Oh no! They're Jerusalem artichokes. Last year someone gave me a handful of roots. We grew them, found them indigestible, had a good laugh and pulled any remaining plants out. We'd heard they were invasive, so I was very careful to eradicate every last trace of tuber, but must have missed some. Now I'm not sure whether to excavate at the risk of destroying the chard bed or let them grow and see who wins. I think I know. Opting to destroy the Jerusalem artichokes, I dig out the roots, trying not to disturb the chard. The invasive tubers sail over the garden fence into the orchard for deer, coyote or raccoon with the hope they'll enjoy them more than we did.

Plum blossoms flutter to the dark garden earth like giant snowflakes. Pink cherry blossoms coat the Japanese garden and a delicate, dreamlike cushion of petals settles on a white chair under the cherry tree. Beneath tall bamboos, blue flowers crest a sea of variegated purple and maroon ajuga leaves; fringed by rings of forget-me-nots, young gingko trees unfold unique shaped leaves; a large black and yellow swallowtail dips and weaves around the last blooming narcissus growing in a salal-covered bank. Sun saturates and warms the spring earth.

Playing in the garden brings optimistic thoughts of the men I met in the valley a couple of weeks ago. Spring is finally here, life is good, and new neighbors are probably enjoying the warm weather as well. Perhaps their wives are gardeners too.

CHAPTER 10

EXPANDING BEES

NO BEES FLY from the kitchen hive this cool morning. I try lifting the hive lid to check on the girls, but the lid is sealed tight with propylis, a resinous substance made from tree sap with strong antibacterial properties. And great sticking power. The bees have worked overtime to glue shut every crack and hole to protect from an unseasonable cold spell. When I finally pry off the lid and peek inside to check on their food supplies, the bees bristle at my intrusion. Hundreds of big black eyes stare up at me. Pissed off. Cuddled near the top of the hive, the warmest place around, they're upset by the uninvited cold air after so many hours of hard work insulating their home. They definitely do not appreciate a stranger poking around. I get the message, replace the lid, and retreat.

But by evening, with warmer temperatures, the much happier bees head straight for garden plum trees as guests at a sumptuous blossom banquet. I watch through a crosshatch of twigs and white petals. Bees hum from flower to flower, each new blossom an open well of nectar. One second for a quick sweet sip through their straw-like proboscis, then off to another flower for another sip, until they're gorged and heavy with a load for the hive. I glance at nearby pear and apple trees, also blooming, but see no honeybees. Plum must be the ambrosia of the hour, winning over all others with the highest sugar content.

With most of the bees grazing contentedly in the orchard, I return to the kitchen hive, squat close to the entrance and watch field bees enter and leave. Some fly out and up at a forty-five degree angle and make a beeline over the treetops to wildflowers in the forest, while others loop around and head in the opposite direction toward the garden, orchard and herb bed. No need for traffic directors here, the bees know precisely where to fly. Returning bees hover in front of the hive, weighed down with pollen and honey, waiting their turn to touch down on the runway. Scout bees dance a complex dance to share up-to-the-minute news of the latest greatest sources of fresh nectar.

Lifting the hive lid is considerably easier since I unglued the barrier of propylis. Rows of burr comb hang from the roof. Burr comb is natural honeycomb that bees create in a tree hole, log, or wall when no beekeeper provides them with commercial frames and wax foundation. Inside a hive, bees will build burr comb if there's a space or a frame missing. In this hive, a feeder rim leaves a wide gap between the lid and top frames and bees have rushed to create burr comb. Cells in the burr comb are ready for eggs and honey storage.

I smoke remaining bees away from the exotic hanging penthouse that already connects to frames in the box below. This year we're trying out liquid smoke spray to avoid stinging eyes and smoke inhalation from billowing, belching, wheezing bellows of an old metal smoker. So far liquid smoke works just as well, a marked improvement over Roy's struggle to light burlap scraps and keep them burning in a strong wind.

The queen has already laid eggs in the burr comb, larvae have hatched and bees have filled some cells with honey. But burr comb doesn't work for modern honey extraction and the comb must go. After scraping the comb from the lid, I take away the feeder rim so the lid fits tightly, with no space for more illegal construction. Roy issues the building permits around here and this wasn't on his list.

Tossing most of the burr comb on the ground near the hive for the bees to rescue their wax and honey for recycling, Roy slices off a dripping chunk to treat us to the season's first honey from neighborhood maple blossoms. Sliding gold and luminous over my fingertips, the honey drips and dissolves to pure sweetness on my tongue. Thank you bees.

☼

The air darts with buzz and hum. Warm weather has activated the bees at Beard's Cove and they're as excited as crowds at a first summer market. Hundreds of field bees hover and dip in front of the hives, waiting to stash loads of nectar and pollen inside the dark frames. Then they turn around and take off right away for another load.

As soon as I'm taped up in my bee suit and veil, a guard bee zooms in to smell whether I am friend or foe. I'm grateful she waited till I was well protected.

We work down rows of hives that Roy re-queened last week to prevent hives from swarming. Hating this brutal aspect of beekeeping, I won't help him when he re-queens. I won't watch him squish the old queen with his hive tool then replace her with a new one. But a young egg-laying queen guarantees abundant brood that translates to good honey production, and a high population colony needs the strength of a young queen's pheromones to keep her subjects loyal. An old or failing queen doesn't produce a powerful enough scent. So the old queens must go. Just not when I'm around.

When we look inside the hives, we're disappointed. Several hives that Roy re-queened have rejected the new queens. We speculate why. Bees in a strong hive will reject a new queen for a number of reasons, but often because they just don't like her scent. Once a hive decides to ignore an introduced queen, or if the hive is queenless for any other reason, they will create their own replacement leader.

Bees choose several less than three-day-old eggs laid by an old queen from which to grow new queens. The cells cradling the chosen 'queen' eggs become supersedure cells where nurse

59

bees care for and feed future queens a high-power diet of royal jelly as the future queen transforms from egg to larva to royalty. As the new queens hatch, they fight each other to death for supremacy of the hive, and the winner, with the strongest pheromones, becomes the colony's new leader. Today, dozens of supersedure cells hang like peanuts from the middle of the frames. The ends of some cells are broken open where new queens have already hatched.

In several hives we can't find a queen. At one hive, a queen cell hatches onto Roy's hand. He cups the baby queen in his palm like a precious gift and escorts her to a hive that has neither queen nor eggs, but just as I lift the hive lid the newborn creeps through his fingers and flies away. Fifteen minutes later, as we inspect another colony further down the row, the runaway queen flies back to Roy and crawls onto his bee suit. She has returned by following her own scent path to its source. Two minutes later she's in a new home ready to lay eggs and be cared for by an adopted family.

At three or four hives the bees are jittery and agitated and scurry in erratic patterns, in contrast to the serene bustle of our healthy colonies. With no queen, bees know their days are numbered when there are no eggs from which to create a new queen. We expect another shipment of queens soon, with luck in time to save these hives. In other hives brood hatches at a spectacular rate, but some of these hives also have no eggs. The queen is either no longer alive or hasn't yet begun to lay. More candidates for young queens. In another queenless hive, workers have begun to lay a haphazard pattern of unfertilized drone brood in the frames.

Field bees zip back to the hives loaded with pollen colored from palest lemon to bright reddish orange. Hind leg pollen baskets bulge from a glut of scotch broom pollen that dusts thousands of hairy backs. Camouflaged golden bees bathe in golden dust in golden petals. The yellow-sunshine invasion of scotch broom in the western states can be traced to just three seeds that germinated in 1850 on Vancouver Island. Broom seed bearers pay attention!

With our work for the day finished, I head to a corner of the forgotten homestead country garden where an overgrown lilac bush is in full bloom. Closing my eyes, I bury my face in the sweet hypnotic fragrance and drift into lilac memories. Even if bees are not enticed by the lilac scent today—they're occupied with the golden storm of broom—I know I am, although I don't think I could do much for pollination.

When we drove home from a market yesterday Roy had a feeling that we should check on the bee yard close to town. The yard was peaceful, with a handful of evening workers bringing honey. But he must have sensed something was brewing.

Today Roy returns from the yard to find that his intuition was correct. Sometime between last night and this morning, a hive was knocked over and the frames scattered. Deep scratch marks gouged the wooden hive body. Bear scratches. The bear chose a dead hive close to the yard entrance, and since the damage was minor Roy thought the bear must have been a young one. A full-grown bear would have torn apart and plundered more than one hive.

A day later Roy checks the bee yard again. When he arrives home his hands and face are red and swollen from dozens of stings. The bear returned to the yard during the night, pushed over a hive full of brood, honey and bees, and dragged boxes into the woods. This was not the work of a young bear. His first trip was only a quick reconnaissance of security measures and defense system, and finding none, the clever bear came back for more serious plunder.

Roy, wearing neither gloves nor veil, picked up an overturned box while bees tried to repair their damaged home. Not a smart move. As soon as he lifted the box to place it back on the hive, bees, hot with memories of bear attack, rushed to defend their devastated home, literally with their lives. And they stung. And stung. Fortunately, after many years of beekeeping Roy's body adjusts quickly to stings.

We return to the bee yard and jerry-rig a bear deterrent for the night: an electrified wire, with sardine treats, stretched across a hole in blackberry bushes where the bear snuck in. We'll have to move the hives from this 'bear yard' as soon as possible before Mr. Bear returns for more chaos and confusion.

CHAPTER 11

RIVER WADING

BEES SMOTHERED in late broom pollen dart home to the kitchen hive to stash their golden riches. As I hike to the river trailhead on the Snake Path, a baby garter snake squiggles under bushes in front of me, another slithers off through the grass; beyond the hive, the tail of a third snake disappears into brush and down a slope.

Grass at the trailhead has leapt breast high. Shasta daisies grin and wave while thistle spikes lash out and scratch through my jeans. The contented buzz of bumblebees rises from trailing blackberry blossoms on the stump pile.

Luminous maple leaf-hands shiver in the sunlight; carpets of tiny white flowers undulate beneath the lacy canopy; diamond water beads sparkle in fan-shaped vanilla leaf plants. Vanilla leaf, when dried and hung in bunches, will fill a home with the sweet spicy fragrance of its name.

The woods are a barely recognizable jungle of burgeoning green. So much has changed so fast since my last visit. Warm days have escalated the unstoppable growth of early summer. The sword fern forest reaches my hips, unfolding upwards forever. Crowds of bleeding hearts and spindly-stemmed Siberian miner's lettuce wave white starflowers under the ferns.

The forest mantle overhead dresses in total green, the shadowy air wet and alive with flying insects.

At the river beach a long-beaked water bird swoops downstream above the surface of the river, her swept back wings and tail feathers in perfect aerodynamic balance as she sounds a rising call from low to high–durweee, durweee, durweee–then vanishes round the bend leaving only a vivid impression of elegant flight, precise mottled feather markings and a long fishing beak.

With every visit to the river a creature, bird, plant, insect or rock that I haven't seen before surprises me. Often, my receptivity is first drawn only to the familiar, maybe in a different angle of light or shadow: fresh dew on an opening leaf; a flower petal illuminated by early morning sunshine; a baby fish darting out from under shadow of a rock; a relative of a garter snake basking at sunset. My awareness broadens as I celebrate subtle shifts of the known. Then, before the end of my rambles, I always receive the gift of something thrilling and unknown, as the woods and river valley share more and more of their wildness and wonder.

Fears about the new neighbors have subsided. I haven't seen them in the woods since my unsettling encounter and they keep quiet in their clearing above the river valley. Perhaps my meeting with them was just a lesson for me to see how attached I had become to my selfish ideal of privacy.

My pace is small, slow and inward as I wander the river shore. I examine beach rocks and contemplate how the rocks live at a slower pace than I could ever imagine, measured in aeons and millions of years. I am humbled, completely insignificant. From a rock's point of view, humans appear and disappear in less than the blink of an eye. I stretch my thoughts to wonder at how long it's taken for them to be molded to what they are now. How much they have seen. How much they could tell. I will pay attention to their stories more closely.

Drawn to the stones' muted shades of subtle gray and beige, some round, some cracked, mottled, speckled, veined, mostly water-washed smooth, I run my fingertips over the rocks, stroke and hold various shapes and sizes. Some feel a perfect smooth fit for my palm while others are lumpy, awkward and strange. Memories arise of many happy hours I've spent on beaches in the company of fascinating, friendly pebbles.

Crooked-legged water boatmen zig and zag across the surface, leaving a trail of ringed mini-wake after each sudden lunge. On the beach a leggy two-tone gray rock spider skitters among two-tone gray pebbles, her veined belly bulging with a brood of beach babies.

Crowds of plants wrestle through gaps between the pebbles. Two types of saxifrage spring from the sandy soil: a piggyback plant with rusty flowers like fairytale oriental slippers; and creamy fringe cup with frilly bell-shaped blossoms. I crouch and pick a wild mint leaf by the water's edge, crumble and roll the leaf between my fingers and inhale the piercing cool fragrance.

The cold current laps against my yellow rubber boots as I wade through shallow water toward a pebble island behind the logjam. Crows squawk in the treetops. Standing still in the current, I relax into animal watchfulness and listen, ready for any signal that calls my attention from the periphery of my senses. Water bobs and ripples around me, painted by reflections of maple, fir, blue sky and overhanging brush. Sounds fluctuate with rising and falling scales of nearby trickles and the distant tumble of water dropping through small rapids downstream. I stoop to cup drops of river water. My hand veers magnetically to the streambed to rest on a piece of maroon jasper the size and shape of a human heart. Cradling the stone in the palm of my hand, I'm led to the beat of my own heart slow dancing with the rhythm of the river.

A deer drinks from the shore upstream, on the other side of the logjam. Startling at my presence, she jumps back up the beach, turns her body toward the woods, but her head and dark eyes hold a steady gaze in my direction.

As shadows grow longer I sink onto the pebbles and let the calm evening seep even deeper inside my skin. Although the beach and river are already shaded, sun-gilded treetops reflect wavering gold on the water. Last sun rays slide slowly up the luminous foliage and the bright river dims to a shadowed murmur.

The deer on the far shore holds her yoga pose, without a blink or nod of an ear, as she watches me wide-eyed for more than ten minutes. Talking to her softly, with no idea what she thinks, I want her to know that I am friendly.

Baby salmon wiggle and squiggle in shallows at my feet. A dusting of insects flits above the undulating water, while behind me, frogs croak louder and louder in the marshes and birds trill serenades to dusk as night eases down the valley floor.

The deer inches up the beach, her head still turned in my direction. I whisper goodbye words to my new friend and leave the riverbank as darkness falls.

With the thermometer at eighty-five degrees, even though still May, it's a shorts-and-t-shirt walk-in-the-water day, away from beekeeping and markets. Roy and I pull on felt-soled fishing boots, the kind usually worn over waders, but there's no need for waders today. We want cold and wet.

The felt shoes might help with footing on slick river rocks, but they're not the right gear for hiking down the steep river trail. The shoes are more like skis. Laughing wildly, we schuss and stumble down the slippery pine needles and loose leaf mold.

But the felt-soled boots work wonders for confidence in river wading as they grip slick river-bottom rocks. As soon as we step off the beach into the current the cold water refreshes immediately, pours over my boot tops and trickles to my toes with squelching coolness. Grains of sand trickle in as well, a minor irritant compared to the luscious cool water. We head upstream with the assurance of explorers, decked out with straw hats, sunscreen, binoculars, sturdy beaver-peeled staffs, cameras and notebook. Perhaps if we were kids again, or intent on losing ourselves completely in nature for the afternoon, we wouldn't need any of the above. How far we've departed from just being animals exploring in the moment!

We hike diagonally upstream across the river then detour overland to avoid jagged arms of the logjam, splash back into the water and wade to a side stream that joins the river from the east where we climb out and rest under shady branches of an old bear-marked cedar tree, a place long familiar to Roy where he's spent many hours, watching the river in every season. Today the water is vibrant with salmon fry. Piles of otter spraint scatter the river bottom near a half-dismembered crawdad.

After resting, we re-enter the side stream and soon reach open beaver marshlands that stretch upstream for miles. Wading thigh-deep along cool reed-choked channels, our shoulders brush through high river grass. Among the reeds, yellow water iris wave flag-like in the hot slow moving air; full-bloom wild rose bushes sprawl under forlorn cedar snags that stand with feet rotting in the marsh. Beaver have transformed the wide valley from woodlands to wetlands and the rising water is too much for cedar trees whose waterlogged roots slowly drown.

Elemental drifts of air, water, heat and sound melt in a pleasurable fusion. From all directions cool running water sings through the warm air. Rivulets trickle and bubble, deep channels gush and plunge over beaver dams in mini cascades. Water melodies rise and fall. Our leisurely afternoon meander mimics the meander of the waterways.

Beaver dams surround us: newly completed dams, works in progress, washed-out dams, each an attempt to regulate water flow for deeper and deeper pools. Rows of sturdy chewed posts prop well-crafted walls woven from layers of mud-daubed sticks and branches. We wander in beaver heaven.

Hoping that a beaver will surface to greet us, we wade to a pond where Ian saw a beaver earlier this year, but everything is quiet at the glassy pool where they hide the entrance to their lodge under deep water. The beaver could not have chosen a more idyllic location. The compound boasts its own private pool, a sloping sandy beach, a lush jungle of food and a big-leaf maple that overhangs the water for shade. Today, in the heat, the beaver are either unconcerned by our presence, enjoying the cool depths of an excavated riverbank, or hiding from us in fear as we lounge on the sandy beach of their luxurious private resort.

We wade further upstream, careful not to disappear unexpectedly down deep holes in the channel–our tall walking sticks prove an essential tool for probing unseen depths–then traverse the top of a beaver dam where water has bull-dozed a shallow ledge of silt.

The river spreads a complex system of veins and arteries across the wide valley floor as it probes and flows and splits into dozens of small channels through the reedy landscape. The water feels heavenly, cold and invigorating against my hot legs, soothing the sting of dozens of thistle, nettle and bramble scratches, as well as countless bug bites.

The sun burns in a piercing robins-egg blue sky. Between the water channels, where the former riverbed evolved to dry land, pebbled islands and beaches beckon us to lie under fluttering alders in the full-on summer's day. Succumbing to enchantment by shivering reflections on slow water, we bask in shady bliss with the knowledge that our bees also enjoy the early summer heat, although undoubtedly hard at work and at a much faster tempo.

A loud plop echoes from a pond upstream. A beaver! I leap to my feet, maneuver across the top of a dam, drop down and wade into a side stream hoping to catch a glimpse of the elusive animal in its wild and natural environment. Camera poised, I am ready and excited to see my first beaver. But as I approach the pond, I step on something strange–not wood, or water, or vegetation–and recognize the familiar crunch of an aluminum can. I am reminded that this land is not only private beaver habitat. We have neighbors.

A moment later I glimpse a human figure hiking through trees in the distance. Of course! Any sane animal would have the same idea: to spend the heat of the afternoon as close to water as possible. Minutes later, there's a loud splash as the man plunges into clear waters of a deep beaver pond, the most natural way to be human on a day like today.

The afternoon almost over, we wade slowly downstream to our land. Climbing back up the river trail slope in our felt wader boots is far easier, though not as hilarious as our descent. Wet felt hooks on the soles cling to the path like sealskin on cross-country skis.

We detour around the Snake Trail, stopping at the kitchen hive to place a small stick between the top box and the lid for ventilation. The temperature inside the hive must be over one hundred degrees.

A perfect newly shed snake skin, thirty-three inches long, lies across the path. What better day to lose an extra layer of clothes.

CHAPTER 12

SWARM SEASON

A NEAR GLOBAL infestation of varroa and trachea mite has destroyed almost all wild honeybees, and an early summer swarm that leaves the relative safety of a hive may not survive the winter. Honeybees must be treated with care and protected against parasites, and now disastrous commercial beekeeping practices and environmental hazards have weakened bees' immune systems drastically, leaving them vulnerable and unable to combat new fungi and viruses that have resulted in CCD, Colony Collapse Disorder.

And since Africanized honeybees arrived on the beekeeping scene, a whole new set of rules applies. Fortunately in the cool Pacific Northwest we haven't yet had to deal with the Africanized bee, but that could change fast if a renegade swarm hitchhikes north from California under the axle of a semi.

A co-op of brave young beekeepers in New Mexico, where Africanized bees have become the norm, wisely welcome the vigor of this 'super strain'. As the feral bees crossbreed with weaker bees, healthier stronger colonies evolve, able to withstand increasingly virulent diseases. Plus they produce a high yield of honey. One drawback of this new breed of super bees is that they strongly dislike loud sounds and any animals that breathe out CO_2. So stay a safe distance away and be quiet!

70

Honeybees, having existed on the planet for millions of years, are fighting back to evolve and pollinate this earth for a few million years more, despite global warming and CCD. They will continue to fill the honey jars for Pooh. Maybe they'll even outlive humans.

☼

As soon as we near the Beard's Cove bee yard to check on the bees, we know something's up, hearing the changed sound even before we witness the main event.

Buzz volume reverberates, swells and vibrates the air above the hives as a tornado-like pillar of bees blackens the sky with thousands of darting insects spiraling upward in a dark cloud.

Swarm season!

The swirling funnel gyrates away from the bee yard toward branches of the nearby weeping willow. I watch, endlessly fascinated by the drama of a colony on the move. After several minutes, the thundercloud of bees begins to rain downward. Hovering and landing on willow twigs, branches and blackberry leaves, most of the bees end up in a milling fuzzy mass. But many more are confused. Where is the queen? Usually when a hive swarms, the queen flies alongside her workers, then when she lands, they hurry to form a protective ball around her. But these bees don't know where to land as they scatter and settle at random over widespread leaves and branches to rest and reconsider their next move.

Roy clacks two tin cans together—a modern variation of old copper swarm-caller paddles—to entice bees down from higher branches. The swarm responds by moving lower but still won't form a cohesive ball. Suspecting the queen may have chosen to stay in the hive, Roy fetches a new queen from the pickup and tapes her little cage to a branch in the middle of the furry melee. But the swarming bees pay no attention to the new queen. They slowly form a ball on another willow branch as they reconnect with their own queen after being temporarily confused by her weak pheromones.

I walk around the perimeter of the yard, scan overhanging trees and discover two more swarms, these ones already well settled. The first hangs in a large oblong shaped ball in a blooming lilac bush, choosing a beautiful aesthetic setting among the purple blossoms. Maybe, like me, the bees enjoy the scent. Another swarm of four drooping curtains sways from a nearby scrubby bush.

Swarms will rest in a temporary location for a day or two while they send out scouts to search for a more permanent habitat, so, leaving the swarms to hang where they are for now, we tend to the more urgent work of prevention of further hive defection by swarming. In this hot weather hive populations multiply fast and if we don't give the bees extra room they'll rush to swarm from cramped living quarters.

Single box hives become two-story condos as we add a layer of deep boxes. We take off feeder rims, scrape burr comb from hive lids and exchange two frames of bees and brood from full bottom boxes with two empty frames from the top box. All the hives are healthy except for two whose populations dwindle with no queens to lay new brood. Roy gives one hive a new queen but not the other. The second hive will re-house a swarm.

While we work, a fourth swarm pours out of a hive, all buzz and agitation. The whirlwind bee storm spirals to the outer edge of the yard, swirls to a tall fir and settles on a branch about twenty feet up.

Even with the excitement and noise of millions of bees flying like tracer bullets in crossfire, the atmosphere is strangely calm and unthreatening. Not a single guard bee has buzzed my veil and none have bumped into my large bulky presence. We are not the focus of the day. Swarming demands the bees' total attention. Before leaving home the bees gorge themselves with honey, become heavy, docile, and solely concerned with protection of their queen during the upcoming migration. Full, fat and ready for the stress and adventure of relocation, they couldn't care less about stray beekeepers.

☼

Roy picks up Ian from school and the three of us transform to swarm patrol commandos. Our ambitious goal: to recapture as many of our truant bees as possible.

The track from highway to bee yard has changed from a nondescript dirt road to a dazzling green tunnel with a floor of tall grass and walls and ceiling of leafy jade. Swarms could be hiding anywhere in the overflowing leafiness of early summer. Carpets of herb Robert and buttercup fringe the overgrown track; greenish blossoms topple from six-foot high nettles; salmonberry flowers drop bright petals to unveil shiny green berry clusters. Zooms and swoops of hummingbirds slice the flight paths of thousands of bees.

We spot yet another swarm we hadn't seen before high in a fir, about thirty feet up, looking very settled and at home. The swarm, hanging there at least two days, presents an interesting challenge for this intrepid band of swarm collectors.

Picture three people dressed in bulky white protective clothing as if about to step onto the moon, equipped with ladder, ropes, boxes, and a broom at the end of a very long handle, as they figure logistics of how to round-up thousands of flying insects from twenty and thirty feet up and fifteen feet out from the center of a large fir. Swarm capture rates as one of the more adventurous, challenging, fascinating and often comical aspects of beekeeping. Humor works well when snatching swarms.

Hiving the more accessible swarms first, we leave the fir tree enigma for later. The first low swarm is easy. While Roy holds a bottom box, with three frames removed, under the dangling furry ball, Ian jerks on the branch to shake loose the bees. Thousands of bees, including the queen, plummet into the hive beneath. We quickly replace all the frames. Since a small clump of lingering bees clings to pheromones left on the branch while a handful fly around disoriented, we leave the hive open so stray bees can follow the scent of the queen to their new home. One swarm down.

The second and third swarms are also easy catches. Roy positions boxes under the swarms while Ian pulls down boughs and I tug on branches to dislodge the hanging balls.

"Now for the higher swarms. I'll hold the ladder. Ian, you climb up into the fir," announces Roy.

Ian pales. "What! The swarm's thirty feet up! Dad!"

"You can make it, no problem," I encourage him, hiding my concern for his safety. We all laugh nervously.

"You can do it! Go for it dude!" adds Roy.

Ian's slender white clad figure disappears up the ladder into the heart of the fir, then shimmies further up the trunk on branch footholds. He tiptoes out on a flimsy limb, tightly grips the overhead swarm branch with both hands and pulls the branch down with all his weight. The fuzzy swarm ball sways crazily. Ian teeters and wobbles. I hold my breath. The limb he's standing on bends low. I listen for the slightest creak or crack.

Roy throws a rope over the swarm branch and lowers it further. I jump up and grab the branch tip. Ian quickly retreats to the main trunk, noticeably relieved, as we are too, when he hugs the sturdy core of the tree. Roy and I shake the swarm branch fiercely. Gentle hum crescendos to loud buzz as a bee avalanche somersaults from the round ball into the waiting hive box.

But our attempted coup is too late. The bees have begun to build honeycomb. Although chunks of bee-covered comb fall to the ground, drooping ridges stay stuck to the branch. We scoop as much comb and as many bees as we can into a waiting hive but doubt that we've dislodged the queen. Bewildered bees crawl on the ground by the box. Clouds of bees fly back to circle around remnants of the hanging comb and the hypnotic scent of their queen. The nest is already too firmly attached to the tree limb for an effective swarm capture. This time the score is: bees-one, beekeepers-zero.

We shift attention to the lower swarm on the same tree, and, with far less drama, grab the limb and give it a quick yank and a shake. The hanging ball falls straight into a waiting box. Immediately bees congregate at the hive entrance and fan with their wings, a good sign the queen is home. The bees' fanning sends out her scent to guide lost or confused bees to the new hive. Perhaps wandering bees who left the higher branch will join the new queen, but it is more likely that the higher swarm will regroup and choose to head for the wild. Hopefully the brave group will survive to pollinate the surrounding countryside.

Four out of five swarms is a good ratio of honeybees who will now stay loyal to our cause as long as we closely watch their escapist tendencies. We congratulate ourselves on an almost completely successful round-up campaign but must play our part as generous landlords and give the bees extra hive space to expand fast growing populations in this time of plenty.

☼

Ashen clouds pile overhead as I head to the valley floor before rain. Deer tracks mark the trail along the riverbank, followed by dog paw prints and then human footprints. Now I know why Zap barked anxiously yesterday evening after a loud gunshot. A poacher. Was the poacher one of our new neighbors? Did they shoot the deer I spoke to last week?

A small branch snaps behind me as I turn toward the river. I quickly look over my shoulder but there is no one there. Then I see three six-inch parallel lines freshly carved into an alder trunk by the path. What do the markings mean? The alder is on our land. The tree cuts cast a sinister shadow on the day. Am I being stalked?

A shot. I jump. The blast from upstream isn't target practice and it isn't hunting season. Zap barks from the top of the bank. Then eerie silence. It is not a friendly day to wander alone by the river. I retreat up the hill. Halfway up, for about twenty feet, I smell a sweet scented smell that reminds me of fruit pies baking in an oven. I have no idea where the smell comes from. I won't investigate.

☼

On his way home from checking hives at Beard's Cove, Roy stops to chat with our neighbor Sharon from the horse ranch across the road. A pit bull has been harassing her horses and she believes someone intentionally let the dog out. She raises four young grandchildren on her own and worries both for the safety of her children and her animals.

I have met the pit bull that belongs to the new neighbors. The dog is not friendly. Whenever I walk past the end of their driveway to hike on Tall Trees Trail, he rushes up barking, bares his teeth, and then stops abruptly at an invisible fence. The new neighbors are not friendly either. They stay to themselves and don't smile or wave when we pass them on the road. Perhaps someone in the community should introduce themselves and welcome them to the neighborhood. But no one wants to. Not with a snarling pit bull to greet the welcoming committee.

PART 2

SUMMER

CHAPTER 13

BEAR AND EAGLE

AT 4:30 AM the predawn sky fills with trills and queees of birds welcoming the long day ahead. Within the hour the first peach glow streaks a partially cloudy eastern horizon. Two robins peck the lawn for a wormy breakfast while a sapsucker taps and sucks at a nearby mountain ash. I'm reminded of the woodchuck tongue twister with a slight change of words: 'How much sap could a sapsucker sap if a sapsucker could suck sap?' For hours the small woodpeckers will drill holes around a trunk to release the sap, sometimes killing a tree by sucking their own food source dry.

For two nights Zap has barked in the direction of the river. He is barking at one of three possibilities: coyotes, a bear, or neighbors, none of whom I'd care to meet. Recently my walks to the river have become less frequent, but this morning, feeling courageous, I take advantage of a quiet hour to follow the trail over the bank.

Tracks etch the muddy bottom of a gully parallel to the main river. Deer tracks. Followed by large animal tracks. Bear? Cougar? Neighbors? Sasquatch? The tracks are bigger than a dog's, not human, and not coyote, raccoon or beaver. I rule out neighbors and Sasquatch. The paw pads are palm-size with four toe prints pointing forward at the end and another toe further down also pointing forward. The tracks are fresh. Now I know why Zap barked. A black bear? A large wild cat? My guess is bear, and from the depth of the muddy imprints I estimate the animal's weight to be three to four hundred pounds. The riverbanks are bear heaven with salmonberries and wild raspberry bushes.

My heart beats faster. My senses sharpen. Is this hulk watching me right now? I scan the densely overgrown bushes where a wild animal has the advantage of familiar habitat, keener senses, plus hunting skills. I wade clumsily to a river island and face the shore. The tracks head north upstream and the wind blows from the south so the bear could smell my scent. If it's a female I hope I'm not between her and her cub, but as there are no smaller tracks, I trust that the bear is alone. I search the high leafy wall of bushes and vines along the shoreline and wonder if a pair of eyes follows my every move. First neighbors, now a bear.

Feeling vulnerable and slightly fearful, I soon relax into the rhythm of water flowing around my island perch, my mood shifting as I become just another animal in nature by the river. And anyway, the bear probably doesn't want an encounter either. But I do keep a watchful eye as I re-cross the river and return home.

Roy identifies my photos as black bear tracks. Around here, a mama bear only attacks if someone stands between her and a cub, disappearing any other time at the slightest whiff of a human. If a bear misses the scent and stumbles across a human by accident, they'll leave right away. In these berry-filled forests black bear are seldom hungry, and they don't hunt humans. But finding yourself between a mama and her cub can be serious. If you're ever in this predicament, you'll hear the mama bear bark a loud grunt to warn the baby to high tail it up a tree. At the sound of the grunt, evaporate. Immediately. If the bear chases you, run faster than you've ever run. Run for your life. If mama catches up and swats you, go limp and play dead.

It could save your life. Do not fight. Do not stand your ground. Let go, relax completely, play dead and pray. There might be maul marks, rips and tears from sharp claws, but if you make her believe she has finished you off, mama will leave to tend to her cub. I hope I never have to practice the previous advice.

Bear have suffered with the decrease in salmon, encroaching development and increased visitors to the region. Recently, as the forests disappear, more bears have been sighted closer to town. They usually 'own' a territory of approximately one thousand acres, but roam several miles. I wonder whether the bear by the river is the same bear who plundered our hives close to town (about nine miles away). Maybe he's come to visit the joker who zapped him with an electrifying meal not long ago.

I have a feeling we haven't seen the last of bear this summer.

From a high snag above the Union River a papa eagle surveys the countryside while, fifteen feet below, a mama eagle perches on the rim of a nest. Something wonderful is happening. The birds are proud and majestic, as any new parents should be, as they watch over their brood.

A week later, the eagle's nest is gone.

Last night, when we drove home from a farmers market, I glanced up and saw one of the eagles perched at the tip of the snag, but didn't see the nest. Dusk cast long shadows, we drove fast, and leaves obscured the view, so I could have been mistaken.

But I wasn't mistaken. Returning this morning we see that only a tiny piece of nest is still attached to the main trunk. A small earthquake struck yesterday morning, followed by strong winds. The quake must have weakened and snapped dead branches cradling the precarious structure, then the nest disintegrated when the high winds blew.

For several weeks we had watched activity at the nest and were sure that eggs had hatched. One of the eagles would perch on the nest rim to give babies space to move around while her mate kept lookout from above. And Roy had seen the mama feed her young as she moved from one side of the nest to the other.

Now the birds and nest are gone and I feel deeply saddened. A mated pair of eagles choosing to build a nest and raise a family so close to town had filled me with optimism.

Without hesitation Roy decides we must search for eaglets that might be lying injured under the tree. The nest fell perhaps eighteen hours ago and as long as there's the slightest chance of survival for the baby birds, we will do whatever we can to rescue them.

With heavy rain bouncing off the busy highway, we stride up and down the shoulder in our waders, carrying a machete and a burlap bag, as we figure out how to reach the eagle tree about two hundred yards away. Not such a great distance. But between us and the cedar tree lies a wet barricade of brush, masses of creeping vine, big leafed bushes, a steep drop to the river, a swift current, deep sucking mud, thick jungle and a dense tangle of fallen branches. Amazing that we are less than half a mile from town.

Choosing a small gap in the bushes, we embark on the rescue mission. Armed with flashing machete, Roy swashbuckles ahead through the dripping thicket to the riverbank where we slide like otter down the slippery slope, treacherous from today's heavy downpour. At the swollen river we sink carefully into the fast waste-high water and wade downstream. Currents race around us. Holes in the riverbed could, without warning, drop away to ten feet deep with water pouring into our chest high waders to sink us like stones. But we move slowly and cross to a shallow sandbar without mishap. Between the sandbar and the far bank, an old fallen tree spans the river. Inch by inch, we ease our slick bodies onto the slimy trunk and squirm over, between, and along dripping limbs to touch down in a deep pool of sucking mud on the far side. A forest of giant skunk cabbage that loves the muck dwarfs all other plants with glossy two-by-three foot foliage. We slurp and heave out of the quagmire onto the riverbank.

Then comes the jungle challenge. Roy slices through over-arching vicious-spiked inch-thick-stemmed brambles. He hacks a makeshift path through tough twelve-to-fifteen-foot incestuous stands of invasive Japanese knotweed. Our very own tropical jungle of Zaire in temperate Washington State. Then, stumbling across the usual deadfall, moss branches, nurse logs and tangled underbrush of a Northwest forest floor, we edge closer and finally make it to the clearing under the old cedar tree. Splattered eagle droppings coat the ground like a blanket of snow; twigs and sticks from the shattered nest lie scattered around. We scan the soaked undergrowth.

Moments later Roy exclaims softly: "Oh wow! Oh wow! A baby eagle."

I rush to where Roy crouches beside a crumpled bundle of feathers lying twenty feet from the trunk. The bird's fluffy chest trembles slightly and there's a glimmer of hope in the weak heartbeat and tiny breath. Barely alive after a cold wet night on the forest floor, the eaglet is fading fast. It doesn't take long for hypothermia to sink a helpless fledgling used to the warmth and comfort of her mama's nest.

Covering her limp body with my jacket, I do what I can to comfort her, whispering, "It's going to be OK. You're safe. You're going to live." I don't know what else to do. It is a miracle that a hungry predator didn't find her last night. But at this time of year there's no shortage of food for any predator, and she's a lucky bird. Kneeling close to her I softly repeat a stream of comforting words and sounds, sending my energy out to her, while Roy searches the perimeter of the tree for any other survivor. The eaglet, big black eyes wide open, very afraid and as if in pain, stutters little sobbing sounds, slight gasps and shudders, but makes no attempt to move. One of her wings splays out at an odd angle.

In a sudden moment of panic I imagine that the eaglet's parents might be watching, might swoop down and attack the human who interferes with their baby. But the wide-winged birds couldn't penetrate the undergrowth, and even if they did, wouldn't be able to fly back out, needing wide open space to spread their broad wingspans for take off. Which is why the mama eagle hasn't attempted to protect or rescue her young.

After scouring the ground under the tree and nearby undergrowth, Roy returns without finding another bird. We decide to quit the search for now and get help for the one baby we found. I spread out the burlap sack, gently scoop the feathered quake victim into my hands, place her on the rough cloth, folding it snugly around her for security, but with enough room to breathe.

Returning to our pickup, Roy carries the wounded bird back across the river and up the slope. Previous tough trail blazing pays off with a quick and easy path back to the road. Even water in the river seems to flow with less force.

The two of us must be a strange sight by the highway. Passing drivers stare as we hike along the shoulder to our truck: two bedraggled figures in waders, a man cradling a burlap bundle and a woman, machete in hand, tagging along behind.

The baby eagle is no small, cute, fluffy, sweet thing. She is a big, scruffy, mite-ridden being with overtures of power, with talons and sharp claws already an inch-and-a-half long, a powerful overhung beak and beginnings of sleek black feathers. At approximately five weeks old, the eaglet is the size of a small turkey weighing about seven pounds, but not mature enough to fly or leave the nest, and now completely helpless with her bent and bedraggled wing.

Every motherly instinct I have wells up. I sit in the pickup with the injured bird nestled on my lap for the next two hours. Snuggling under the covers with her head tucked close to her battered wing, she's motionless except for a slight rise and fall of mottled chest feathers and a flutter of heartbeat. She's been quiet through the whole ordeal but now there's the faintest catch in her breath and I hope she hasn't caught cold. Slowly, she warms up and seems to be fast asleep but when I carefully lift a corner of the blanket, a wide-open dark eye stares back at me.

Truck windows steam up from the warmth of our resting bodies as heavy rain pours down outside. I sink into mild euphoria as I coddle the baby eagle on my lap like a nursing mother, with my heart warm with gratitude for my role in her rescue. I peek under the covers and take in the details of her young body: light brownish-gray fuzzy thighs, downy under-feathers, quill-like beginnings of wing feathers, small black head and neck feathers. And talons.

We drive to the Theler Wetlands Project where the director calls around to find out where we should deliver the injured bird. I realize that while everyone else, all males, refer to the eagle as 'he', I am the only person calling it 'she'. It is too young, except for an expert, to tell what sex it is, but I continue to call it 'she'.

We contact a wildlife shelter an hour's drive north, on Bainbridge Island, run by an eagle expert who returns injured birds to the wild after their recovery. She tells Roy to put the bird in a cardboard box and bring it in. At first, I cannot bear to put the eaglet in a cold box to bounce around in the back of the pickup. It feels right for the injured bird to snuggle against the warmth and comfort of my body. But the woman has explained to Roy that if the eaglet lies on a flat surface, the bird will wiggle around to find the most comfortable position for her injured wing, which she might not try if held by a stranger. This makes sense, so when I feel she's well rested, warm, perked up a bit and beginning to move, we pull over and put her in a cardboard box. As I put the box on the bed of the pickup she pokes her head above the lid with a sharp eagle-eye questioning stare as if to say:

"What's going on NOW, and where are YOU going!"

She is regaining her true eagle spirit. I will never forget the soul communication transmitted through her deep black eyes in that gaze filled with every heartrending emotion of bonding and leaving, as coming together and parting become one.

By the time we reach the shelter, the eaglet is in much better shape than when we found her. The shelter director, a soft-spoken compassionate woman, swiftly takes charge and confirms that the young bird has a fractured wing. She lifts the eaglet carefully by the legs to avoid the sharp claws, wraps her in a soft swaddling cloth and performs a healing hypnosis.

The bird will be kept under observation overnight, rest for two days to stabilize from the trauma and then be flown to Eastern Washington for surgery and rehabilitation. The goal is for her eventual return and release to the wild, close to her home. The flight to Eastern Washington will be courtesy of an airline that flies eagles for free. The eaglet is in safe hands.

Even before we arrived at the shelter the director had arranged a search party of a dozen people to scour the ground beneath the cedar tree where the eagle nest had fallen. She guesses that another baby could have landed as far as 180 feet in any direction.

We stop on our way home to talk to the search party. They haven't yet found another bird, so Roy re-crosses the river to join their search as I wait under a dripping big-leaf maple. Reflecting on the instinctive bond between different species when one of them is in trouble, I feel elated and honored to have helped save a bird sacred to Native Americans, a spiritual link between earth and air and the national symbol of America. Perhaps I've even accrued a little good 'eagle karma'.

Dusk slides to darkness and the rescue search is called off till daylight.

☼

Two days later I drive past the tree where the eagle nest fell and look up. One of the parent eagles perches on the topmost branch. Hoping to ease the anguish of a bereft parent, I send a silent message that one of their babies is safe but in somewhat strange surroundings.

The next day Roy has bad news. The animal shelter x-rayed the eaglet and found a shoulder broken beyond repair as well as the fractured wing. The baby eagle has been put to sleep.

Although the eagle rescue has no happy ending, after the initial disappointment I know that I've been blessed by the gift of my intimate time with the bird. We did everything we could and we're grateful that she didn't suffer a slow, fearful, cold death from hunger, or by the sharp teeth of a predator.

CHAPTER 14

EARLY TAHUYA SUMMER

LONG OVERDUE for a rendezvous with the mower, the foot high lawn bends from last night's heavy soaking. Drenched wild grass in the orchard reaches my hip. Bushes and blossoms struggle, bruised and storm-battered. Pastel apple and magnolia petals dangle crumpled, smeared and streaked like the skin of an aging actress whose tears have etched pathways through cheap make-up. Gaudy trashed azaleas hang limp above a mass of doubled-over columbine that crushes a bed of sweet William below.

The soaked garden sprouts. And sprouts. First bean leaves erupt into the daylight and a row of small bumps herald another row. But next to one beanpole, a mound larger than my fist, closer to the size of a soccer ball, is about to break the surface. Can Jack's beanstalk compete with this champ about to explode? Is there a pot of gold on the horizon? Are garden gremlins playing games with me? I don't remember planting a bean seed the size of a golf ball. But then, of course! This is the work of a mole, one of many who sup on worm buffets in fertile soil around the yard. No pot of gold this summer.

Perennial poppies wear fuzzy caps over the first hint of red petals. In the herb bed, chives wave sunburst spikes and thyme flowers froth over a low bush next to a forest of parsley. First tiny cherries, soon to be bird food, dangle from a cherry tree.

☼

A female pheasant struts through an overgrown ditch by the driveway, looking like a large grouse with her camouflage of mottled brown feathers. Suddenly, behind her, seven or eight baby chicks appear, about two weeks old, scurrying through the tall grass. We stop the pickup. Mama pheasant stops. Her babies skitter ahead in the open, blissfully unaware of potential danger. But Mama knows best. Her sharp tongue chirps to the chicks who understand the urgency of her call as they stumble and flip-flop over each other in a dash for cover.

In the fall, pheasants are freed in the Tahuya forest for hunters, with release dates and hunting times listed in the newspaper. Perhaps 'freed' isn't the right word since most birds die within the first hour of the one-sided sport. They don't stand a chance. For years the game department released only male pheasants but now, for every three cages of males, they release one cage of females. A few, very few, lucky birds dodge the hunter's gunfire and escape to the refuge of our land, and even fewer survive the winter. Having been fed by humans since birth they're not raised to survive in the wild. This mama pheasant and her chicks are true survivors.

We drive a back road to the mouth of the Dewatto River by the Hood Canal. The road, in use since early days of horse and cart, winds to sea level through a floating leaf-ocean of giant big-leaf maples, fir and cedar, enveloping us in a sea of healing green.

The healing green is essential. Interspersed with the cool green beauty of the trees, recently stripped hillsides have left the earth scarred and bare. A couple of old homesteads where early settlers cleared land, planted orchards and subsistence crops, are now Christmas tree farms lined with straight row fields of perfect small conical trees that will be harvested in five or six years for export to lucrative Japanese markets.

There's almost no traffic on the road, and what traffic there is, speeds by far too fast. When we pull over and park by the road above the river, first one, and then another pickup swerves past, racing to their destination. Do the drivers, who perhaps take this route every day, drive recklessly with eyes straight ahead to avoid seeing the ravaged landscape?

At a shady campground, where a small creek runs into the Dewatto River, shawls of moss and lichen drip from cedar branches. A spectacular fern headdress, like an Amazon chieftain's feathered crown, towers above the crest of an eight-foot cedar stump that overlooks the campground. Only one camper occupies a shaded campsite even though it's almost summer. And he is hidden away in a travel trailer equipped with all modern conveniences. Summer isn't predictable this time of year, and this camper, while playing it safe, is at least enjoying a day almost close to nature.

The Hood Canal, a fjord, glowers dark and deep. On the far shore, Olympic foothills rise fast and steep from the western shoreline, carpeted by evergreen forest and the inevitable poorly shaved clear cuts. Above the foothills, jagged snow-patched rock juts against a steely sky. Measured by aeons of geologic time, the jagged Olympics are young mountains.

Driving home, we explore back roads and hidden ponds. The world smells clean and fresh after a night of hard rain. But the forest back roads are not clean. Litter fills ditches. And not the occasional Styrofoam cup, water bottle or beer can. Tires, chairs, sofas, rusted appliances, TVs and computers have ended their lives in back road dumping grounds. Ripped garbage bags spew disintegrating paper, bottles, plastic, diapers and mounds of unidentifiable soggy muck tossed out at the beginning of the twenty-first century. Birds and curious animals have scrounged through and scattered what must seem to them an intriguing mess hoping for a treasure, but it is more likely that this intriguing mess is a cruel hazard to their health.

Streams gush through culverts under the road and cascade into mysterious deep gullies. Clumps of sword fern rush from steep embankments to camouflage debris with a fast growing undergrowth of beauty. As we drive further into a maze of half-overgrown dirt roads, less litter shows up, although even in the most hidden places we stumble across traces of a brush picker's lunch from a grocery store cooler.

We hurry from reminders of human carelessness to a large beaver pond I have renamed Wild Lily Lake. We also hurry to beat dark clouds that threaten a wet afternoon, hoping to admire again pink blossoms of Western bog laurel we had seen last week. But we're too late. The flowers have faded and fallen. At this time of year flowers bloom and die overnight and clouds can open and soak in an instant.

Today, another pink blossom has usurped the floral throne held by last week's bog laurel. Damp woodlands around the lake showcase extravagant ruffles and lipstick-pink glamour of a French boudoir. Sumptuous wild rhododendron blossoms line the path to the water. Like a bumblebee longing to lose herself in a pollen daze, I brush my face along bouquets of wet rhody petals beside the steep path while picture postcard views of the lake appear and disappear through the huge flowers. Floating on the surface of the lake, yellow pond lilies, waxy golden bowls of sunshine, nestle between plate after plate of lily leaves that idle in a stately flotilla.

Closer to the water's edge the calm lake reflects carbon gray from the approaching storm. Silence creeps weightless and eerie over the swampy surface of half-submerged snags, floating lilies and pondweed. I almost expect something lurking and prehistoric to crawl from the murk.

Roy finds a comfortable resting place under a snag full of bird nest holes while I wander off with my camera to explore the lakeshore, following a trail used by small night visitors. Pausing beside a floating chunk of mossy log wedged against washed-up forest debris, something unusual in the damp moss catches my eye.

A fluorescent carnival of miniature Ferris wheels has set up shop on the green bog moss bed! Moisture-drop halos, the consistency of clear glue, cling to tips of red hairs encircling popsicle-shaped yellow leaves, while increasing drizzle glazes the entire bizarre specimen with a luminous shine. Reminiscent of coral or a sea anemone, this round-leaved sundew plant would be more at home on a tropical ocean floor than beside a temperate beaver pond. It's the strangest plant I've ever seen.

The plant looks dangerous. Investigating closer, I immediately know why. The monster eats animals. Dismembered iridescent blue/green dragonfly limbs litter the moss beneath the plant like bones thrown from a medieval banquet. Though the odd organism is probably harmless to humans, I won't risk a finger to find out.

A quick visit to my field guide tells me that sundew devours the same insects that pollinate the oddball insectivore. Now there's gratitude for you! But considering how many plants we humans devour, I really can't fault the plant for taking a bite from higher up the food chain. Both Native Americans and old Europeans believed that the juice from the carnivorous sundew could remove warts, and in Europe the sticky gel was used to set cheese and junkets. The name sundew is derived from sindew, meaning 'always dewy'. The swamp plant collects nitrogen not from the soil, but from doomed bugs that fly too close and crash into its sticky tendril-waving snares. Honeybees beware!

Excited by my unusual find, with rain now trickling down inside my collar, and my camera full of unique shots safely tucked in the shelter of my jacket, I hurry back to where Roy still rests under the bird nest snag. I tell him about my discovery of the carnivore by the shore.

We joke that we wouldn't mind fast-growing patches of carnivorous plants in various key locations. Perhaps we could plant some around remote bee yards to munch on vandals. Or in our neighborhood to discourage the neighbors' pit bull.

CHAPTER 15

JUNE BEEKEEPING

WARM WEATHER forecast for the next three days promises a bonanza of nectar, plus inevitable swarm cells and feisty queens plotting to escape with a swarm. The bees need extra storage frames right away.

We deliver thirty-two shallow supers for the overcrowded hives at Beard's Cove and while unloading, immediately cover the stacked boxes with lids. If bees sniff the irresistible sweetness of last year's honey residue, robbers will rush to the fast-food temptation.

Working first along the back row, we clear hive entrances where tall grass and weeds have shot up, fed by 'compost' dragged from hives. Then, lifting frames to look for tiny egg dots in cells to see if the queen is laying, we check the health of the bees and colony as a whole. The first two hives have no eggs, but strong populations, probably two of the hives that swarmed last week. Roy gives each hive a new queen.

Early summer wraps us with a waving quilt of feathery purple, green and brown grass heads. Pastures glow with reddish sorrel. As we work, the air brims with bee zing, warbler birdsong and the shrill whistle of hummingbird flight. When I raise my head from a hive to look for the hummingbird, my vision fills with the dancing flash and zoom of thousands of mellow bees. Above the swirling insects, a raucous mama crow chases a circling hawk who shows too much interest in her nest.

After long hours of working up and down two rows of hives, I'm hot, hungry, tired and more than ready for a trip into town for lunch. But guard bees harass me for minutes, refusing to quit when all I want to do is take off my bee suit. Two aggressive bees buzz and lunge and bombard me even when I leave the yard to shelter in shady green branches.

I try standing still. I try brushing them off. I try diving into the undergrowth. Nothing works. One bee crawls over the netting in front of my eyes for five excruciating minutes, as she meticulously probes every inch for a gap in my armor. This persistent bee is out to get me and she won't give up until she does. The siege irritates me. I'm tempted to murder my tormenter, but practice restraint, knowing I'm well covered and she will eventually lose interest. I'll outwait her. Finally she leaves for home, followed by the others. The air is quiet again.

But not for long. When I return to the truck and take off my gloves and veil, Zzzzzzzzzz, here they are again. I don't react well to attacking bees when I'm irritable and hungry. Unveiled, I hurry up the path again, but not fast enough. A bee, must be the same persistent one, tangles in my hair, not once, not twice, but three times. Then on her final suicide attack, she jabs her stinger into my cheek just below my left eye, forfeiting her life in defense of her hive, although it feels more likely that she has a personal vendetta. Perhaps I harmed a hive sister.

Poison rushes through nerves in my sinuses, down my neck and around my head. A sting on the hand or arm is bearable, but a head sting is nasty. I dose myself with plantain tincture and take an antihistamine. I don't relish selling at markets looking and feeling like a creature from outer space, a look I know well from a previous sting between the eyes.

I often clumsily kill bees as I replace lids or boxes. A sting warns me to pay attention, treat the bees with more awareness, and watch levels of fear that have occasionally resembled hysteria. Bees smell fear instantly. And in future my veil will stay on my head until I am safely in the truck.

☼

Roy leaves home to clear a bee yard in woods where we've kept bees before, close to acres of huckleberry bushes. He soon returns.

After unlocking a gate (the property is owned by a timber management company) and driving a short distance into the forest, he came across a small beat-up travel trailer parked by the road. He greeted the seedy-looking occupant. The man told Roy he was working with loggers in the woods. But the man didn't fit the picture of any logger Roy ever met, and when Roy dropped the names of timber company personnel, the man's answers didn't add up. Continuing up the road to the proposed bee yard site, Roy soon thought it wise not to stick around, deciding to question the man's identity with the timber company before returning to the new bee yard site. The man could have been guarding illegal activity, perhaps a meth lab.

Timber company staff say they don't know anything about the man or the trailer, but promise to check on the situation. So until then we must wait to move hives. Although the bees thrive in their present location, the larvae-filled boxes are a huge temptation for a hungry bear. We also want to move the bees closer to 'huckleberry heaven' soon for the rich golden huckleberry honey that market connoisseurs repeatedly request.

☼

At the Theler wetlands, high grass almost buries half-a-dozen hives. Shrill red-winged blackbirds swoop over the fresh water marshes; red wings of a dragonfly hold steady on a cattail, while a yellow swallowtail flutters nearby; powder-blue forget-me-nots speckle a buttercup carpet; blue water echoes a cloudless sky. Pollen-dusted bees suck up a storm along an avenue of wild roses. My eyes feast on the luminous rainbow colors of early summer. After many dull days, the welcome sun strokes warm waves across my skin. But later this afternoon the sun will disappear during a forty-percent solar eclipse.

The first beehive at the wetlands is crammed with bees. And swarm cells. But we've arrived in time to prevent a swarm. Roy destroys the queen cells by scraping the hanging peanut-shaped cells from the frames with his metal hive tool and squishes any cells ready to hatch. The second hive shows no hint of swarming. The third hive, which has already swarmed and is queenless, has only a handful of bees crawling over nearly deserted frames.

While Roy works with the third hive, I saunter along a plant-choked ditch photographing bees and flowers. An over-sized bee staggers across the head of a massive cow parsnip blossom. A queen! Bewildered and disoriented, she meanders aimlessly over the creamy lace quilt. Queen bees don't gather nectar from flowers—that's the job description for field worker bees—and this royal wanderer is more than a little confused. She must be newly hatched from a swarm cell from the first hive. I shout to Roy that I have a queen. He runs over with a frame of bees and tries to coax the queen from the flower to the frame, but she can't be coaxed and flies away even more confused. The third hive doesn't get a royal transplant. Perhaps the disoriented queen will survive long enough to mate with drones and then assume her regal egg-laying duties. But first she must find and be accepted into a hive.

Later, the air at the Beard's Cove bee yard is thick with bees at their exuberant best on a summer's afternoon as they zoom home to the hives, heavy with nectar from blossoms, blossoms and more blossoms. Roy and I work silently in a unified rhythm up and down the rows, checking inside each hive and adding more boxes where needed. Which is most hives. Only a couple of previously queenless hives are weak. The girls bring in nectar by the bucketful and stuff it into every available cell not already filled by velvety brood ready to hatch. Within a week the number of bees at this yard will multiply by thousands, possibly millions. The hives are doing exactly what we want: hustling, bustling and bursting with activity.

We are so absorbed in our work that the afternoon eclipse passes unnoticed.

My evening wander by the river feeds many a bug his evening meal. Every insect population explodes in the warm weather. Returning home via the snake path I squat by the kitchen hive, put my ear against the outer wall and thrill to the deep pleasurable throb and hum rising from the depths. A hundred thousand wings fan to dry the liquid gold.

☼

Three messages wait on the answering machine. A man calls to say bees have nested in his mailbox. Unlikely. The 'bees' are probably hornets. The second call is from a woman who describes a round gray 'beehive' under her deck. Undoubtedly hornets. The third caller, close to the wetlands, found a swarm of bees hanging in a tree on his property the size of a basketball, perhaps the same swarm that recently left the now queenless wetlands hive. This is a busy time of year for a beekeeper.

The phone rings again.

A month ago, Roy heard from a woman on the Olympic Peninsula who had bought a hive of bees from him last year. She told a sad tale of bee loss. When she checked on her hive one morning, she found thousands of dead bees on the ground in front of the landing board. All her bees had died and she was sure they had been killed by pesticide poison. Her neighbor owns an eight-acre pasture and she had seen him scatter white powder to rid the earth of moles living in the teeming healthy soil. Since the pesticide kills all bugs, worms and insects leaving a sterile environment with no food for the moles, the moles move away. The systemic pesticide also seeps into flowers where her bees sip nectar. How could the man be so short sighted? The woman, an excellent beekeeper who loves bees and cares deeply for nature, was very upset. Roy told her he would take care of her, promising that at some future time he would deliver replacement bees.

Today Roy listens to a follow-up tale from the woman. Last Friday she was away from home running an errand when her husband heard a loud buzzing from the yard. He glanced out of the window and watched as a gyrating swirl of bees, a swarm, headed for the hive. Over the next hour, bees massed on the hive front and funneled in through the entrance.

Returning home, the beekeeper, before speaking to her husband, noticed a handful of bees flying near her old hive (most bees had already entered the boxes). She thought perhaps they were stray bees robbing honey left by previous tenants, and walked over to examine the hive. When she lifted the lid she was amazed to find two boxes full of contented bees settling into their new quarters.

So she called Roy to ask if it was he who delivered the bees to her hive, since he had promised replacement bees. But Roy had nothing to do with the arrival of the unexpected swarm. Sometimes miracles happen to people who deserve them. The swarm arrived out of the blue. The bees knew exactly who would provide a good home, most likely having absconded from the hive of a nearby beekeeper. I hope they have the sense not to visit the neighbor's meadow.

When I hear the story, I imagine Roy driving around the Northwest like a fairy godmother with his little red pickup packed with bees, dispensing swarms with directions to fly and fill the empty hives of deserving beekeepers.

But the woman needs to adopt a good strategy for educating the neighbor so that her bees will not be poisoned again. She could begin by taking the neighbor a gift of a jar of honey. Then maybe a small apple tree that needs pollination. The pesticide poisoner might get the message. Or not.

CHAPTER 16

GARDEN WEEDS

THE GARDEN explodes with new growth. Again, unwanted Jerusalem artichokes shove hefty stalks through earth reserved for chard and amaranth. Again, I scoop even further down into the dirt and unearth smallest fragments of rhizome scattered by rototiller blades. The unwanted roots sail up and over the garden fence toward the orchard. Let the outcasts grow where their sunflower-like flowers will bloom in fall, or where they'll offer an easy meal for a hungry animal strolling his morning territory.

Poppies have tossed fuzzy coats to unfurl blood-red petals. Inside a silken flower head, erotic purple splashes and powdery stamens protect the womb of the poppy, a greenish ball emblazoned with a raised pink mandala. Within the womb hide seeds of thousands of poppy children.

Yellow flowers of last year's kale flutter in a sunny duet with bees. And bees. With straw-like proboscis they sample a quick sip of nectar here, a quick suck there. The bees dance from flower to flower, touching down only briefly at each blossom, knowing the nectar pool isn't deep and plentiful, but enough for a light snack. The more flowers brushed, the more pollen dusts hairs of the furry visitors en route to neighboring blossoms awaiting the alchemy of pollination. But as soon as the kale flowers finish blooming, most of the plants will be loaded onto the compost pile, leaving only half a dozen stalks for next year's seed.

Last dogwood blossoms flutter across the lawn; azaleas drop red, yellow and fuchsia petals; leaves of cherry, plum, apple and pear shimmy and rustle in layer upon layer of swaying green.

Metal wind chimes by the woodshed improvise resonant clink clank melodies.

I weed the carrot bed. When I calculate weed volume in the bed I'm certain that the package of carrot seeds must have contained seventy-five percent chickweed, grass, peppergrass and other anonymous species, in addition to the real carrots. Every now and then I discover a couple of spiky seedlings topped by the first variegated leaves. What happened to the rest of the seeds? I must trust that as soon as I've routed the carrot impostors, the beds will transform to a feathery headdress ocean hiding an underground forest of orange root.

The orchard is a prairie meadow; red sorrel, clover and daisy flowers flash color through high waving grass blades; purple vetch twines upward to sleek grass seed heads. White blossoms flutter in an apple tree, while below, in the garden, valerian reaches five-feet and opens her heady perfumed pink flower clusters.

A band-tailed pigeon coos a soulful message from fir trees to the north while swallows circle strong wind currents, wheeling in to their nests under workshop eaves. A rufous hummingbird braves sharp gusts to suck last drops of azalea nectar. The distinctive call of a towhee rings through the clearing, a constant accompaniment this time of year, short simple notes every few seconds at steady intervals. I wonder what mantra the towhee repeats all day long.

Mindlessly pulling out grass shoots, I spend an hour in the garden, struggling in a tug-of-war with very long, very stubborn roots from around seedlings now recognizable as tiny parsnip greens, then work down carrot, amaranth and lettuce beds. Tired of weeding, I take an extended break to savor colors and scents of the herb garden: purple chive blossoms, orange and gold marigolds, pale lavender blooms on a thyme bush. Roy plants cucumber starts in the old kale bed while I sit and watch in a garden daze.

Then the thought occurs to me that later this week I'll spend hours at farmers markets standing on asphalt, probably thinking about rebel weeds plotting to choke vegetable beds. I return to the vegetable beds with renewed effort at eviction of obstinate squatters.

☼

Outside the garden fence a row of lupines bloom in pastel pinks and purple. Last winter I over-fertilized the plants courtesy of the horse ranch across the road. Now one stalk shows off thirty-one inches of blossom with purple flowers open all up the stem. The lowest blossoms are starting to wilt, fade and die. Fast. The heat wave of the last two days has accelerated the end of short-lived petals. On the other side of the garden, raspberry flowers have come and gone in a rush, leaving behind fuzzy green-soon-to-turn-red berries.

I feel the firmness of the first round red radish and taste test the tangy flesh. Sapphire blue blossoms radiate from tall delphiniums. Sweet Williams release sweet fragrance. A feisty hummingbird, his tiny heart beating up to five hundred times a minute, zooms in, hovers and vibrates joyfully within three feet of my eyes for a long magical moment. Within seconds: touch, taste, sight, smell and sound.

Waging battles with weeds for hours, I liberate carrot-land, beet-land and the state of parsnip from guerrilla grass. I watch my gleeful imperialist bravado as I uproot and destroy the sneaky enemy. This is my kingdom. Let proletariat weeds proliferate elsewhere. This little patch of earth is reserved for civilized plants: taste-bud-delighting plants, famous plants, with fancy names and catalog photos oohed and aaahed over in thousands of homes across the country. A cow might not agree with my war on guerilla grass, but until we humans have developed a stomach that can digest crab grass, quack grass, witch grass and any other wild and willful grass, I will continue

102

my defense of the veggie beds. Maybe I'm not such a lazy gardener after all.

I inch along the damp ground between raised beds, freeing the beleaguered veggies. The sharp citrus smell of lemon balm drifts from a bush to my left; next, sweet and minty anise hyssop lifts my spirits; a St John's Wort bush with no strong scent but a wild personality exudes optimism; clumps of parsley whisper their characteristic odor; then, last in the row, a mass of oregano evokes memories of herbal aromas wafting from smoky Mediterranean kitchens. The sensory delights of smell distract my mind from the wholesale slaughter of innocent grass blades.

Where did all those blades spring from this year? I don't remember such a battle before. The willful grass rages on, determined to create lawns on the raised beds. Lawns in valleys, lawns up slopes, lawns across raised bed plateaus. Grass fights to own the whole territory. So far I've reclaimed most of the plateaus. Slopes and valleys will have to wait till later.

While I weed, a young deer grazes in the orchard fifteen feet away, completely at ease with my presence. She raises her hind leg to scratch a twitching ear, then goes back to pruning juicy leaves from low branches of an apple tree. Too bad I can't invite her to help me prune garden weeds but I doubt I could teach her the difference between a weed and a cultivated treasure.

In the darkening western sky a crisp new Moon floats close to a bright Venus. I leave the garden and lie, contented and satisfied, on the lawn, the rightful kingdom of grass. Cradling my head in my hands, I close my eyes and watch as armies of grass roots flutter inside my eyelids.

The earth, the plants, the trees are warm and wet in the early morning of a cloudy, sultry day. After many hot days, heavy rains have scarred plants. Flowers are bent over, mourning for lost beauty. Battered roses hang wilted and brown and rain-soaked petals scatter the earth. Last week's heat and bruising downpours accelerate the cycle of death and decay. But the bees are happy to fly out after a day of enforced housekeeping. Dozens of striped girls suck kale blossoms and zip to and fro between orchard clover and herb garden thyme. Lupine seedpods bulge with next year's seed. In the vegetable garden, green becomes greener in a bid to hide every inch of naked earth.

I stroll around the clearing to inventory the latest decorative splashes, renovations, additions and demolitions. Salal bushes line the driveway with pretty pink hanging lanterns while ever-sunny Shasta daisies and dandelion relatives show off everywhere between brown seed heads and ubiquitous bracken.

The deserted chicken coop is a potent mass of vegetation sprung from dirt rich from years of multilayered high-nitrogen fertilizer. The run recuperates from the hens constant pecking at the hard dusty ground with a tangle of pussy toes, shepherd's purse, thistle, fern, daisies, common groundsel, dock, blackberry runners and other robust species that relish every moment of over-fertilized existence. A fine crop of grains, sprouted from stray chicken feed, adds to the chaos. We should have planted vegetables in the coop. Perhaps we will next year, after this year's motley groundcover has completed the hard work of breaking up the tough surface, transforming it into rich humus for veggies.

In the garden, miniature green football Italian plums weigh down branches. Nearby, first yellow rue flowers have opened; a bee favorite, rue blossoms all summer till first frost.

A stately swallowtail, a proud Spanish galleon with sails flapping in the wind, swoops low and almost lands on my forearm to attract attention as I admire red and pink yarrow next to sky-blue delphiniums. She's a beauty. The butterfly whispers in a low provocative voice: "Watch me! Let me pose for you," as she heads straight for the dazzling mass of delphiniums. She knows the dramatic effect of her zebra stripes, dots and spots against the brilliant blue, lit by oblique low sunshine. Lucky I have my camera. The brazen insect shows off her exquisitely designed wide-open wings. She grazes first at one flower for several seconds and then hops to the next. But she knows her boundaries. When I edge too close with the camera, she backs off to blossoms hidden behind stems and flutters briefly around the garden before returning to model in her blue heaven for a second show.

The swallowtail isn't the only insect enjoying the flowering stems this early morning. Dozens of bumblebees commute between delphiniums and penstemon. Two of them circle me again and again, warning me I'm in their territory. Bumblebees usually don't bother me, but this morning's bumble language is more aggressive than usual. I heed the warning and leave what is really my territory. I am not going to argue with them. There's time and space for all of us.

Two long garter snakes, sunning themselves by the kitchen hive close to where I found a snakeskin last week, slither off into the grass at the vibration of my steps. A third snake slides past, and as I walk away, I almost step on a fourth. Near the entrance to their underground winter pit, the earth is alive and crawling with snakes who have chosen to stay close to home after leaving their winter den, on cool days basking on open land close to the warmth of the beehive. I guess too that they hang around there in the hopes of grabbing the occasional low flying bee.

I return to working in the garden between veggie rows, engrossed in yet another weed destruction project. A snake glides out from under at St. John's Wort bush. I appreciate snakes on the path by the beehive, but not slithering over fingers as I weed. I will pay attention to where I put my hands. But snakes are always welcome in the garden for pest control. Just not where I work.

Sitting beside the parsnip bed, picking and plucking, my bare arms brush against something cold and wet. I jump, but no, it is not a snake. The cool refreshing wetness on parsley bushes to my right is bubbly aphid secretion. Aphid nymphs suck on plant juices after they hatch, then envelop themselves in frothy white foam for camouflage and to prevent drying out. Birds and predators choose not to search through the gooey foam for the hidden insect.

Weeding discipline done for the day, I wander around the garden lingering close to dreamy scents of Valerian and rose that conjure expensive French perfumes, spellbinding attractors for pollinators. I gather up an extravagant bouquet of lupine, daisy, sage, yarrow, rue, parsley flowers and bird's foot trefoil. Plus valerian and one fully opened pink and yellow rose.

CHAPTER 17

Fir/t Honey

ROY BRINGS disappointing news after checking on the bee yard in the Olympic foothills west of the Hood Canal. Quilcene is further north and the hives are at a higher elevation than those on the Tahuya Peninsula. Spring has been unusually cold and damp and flowers are late to bloom. The bees, nearing starvation, are reluctant to leave the warm safety of the hive to chase down sparse blossom and as a result, populations haven't expanded, hives are almost honeyless, and the bees have begun to eat their own larvae.

As an emergency measure, even though already summer, we must feed the bees or we might lose them. Recently, we heard from a big commercial beekeeper with hives near the Canadian border, who has had to feed his hives a tankerful of sugar syrup each week. Tomorrow, even though the weather has improved and the bees are out foraging, we'll take buckets of sugar syrup to save the stressed Quilcene hives. The more food on the table, the more the queen will lay to avert disaster in low population hives.

Fog shrouds the summer morning. But the forecast promises that clouds will burn off early, with temperatures rising above 70 degrees. By the time we cross the floating bridge at the north end of the Hood Canal, the fog dissolves to a postcard panorama of Olympic Mountains splashed with dirty snow. Then the high mountains disappear as we drive into the foothills and disappear in the rolling jade slopes.

We stop at the orange gate to timber management land and switch on our CB radio. Meeting a logging truck careening down the steep winding road as we head up to the bee yard is not in our plan for the day.

"Hello. We're beekeepers in a small red pickup coming up the hill. Over."

"Pull over! Wait! Four loaded trucks just left the logging site on their way down."

Lucky we turned on the radio. As the message ends, a massive truck looms around a bend, grinds and snorts down the narrow track, thunders and quakes the ground with a full load of timber. Fifty tons of screeching machine and leafless, limbless trunks of valuable sheltering conifers.

The first truck passes. When the earth has stopped trembling, before the next truck, we have time to drive to a fork in the road where we turn away from the direction of the massacre. Everything is quiet again, but an invisible pall lingers over the hillsides.

As we climb in elevation we pull over every hundred yards to observe honeybees on blossoms. Finally the weather is warm enough for the bees to fly and we hope it isn't too little, too late.

Bee populations at the yard are dangerously low. Cold weather has taken its toll and dead bees litter the ground in front of some of the hives. But the tide has turned. A soft buzz vibrates the air outside the bear fence where dozens of native bumblebees, plus a handful of honeybees, hover around creeping blackberries and clover between tire tracks on the road to the yard.

But it will take a miracle for these bees to make a comeback to produce extra honey for us to harvest this year. These hives are too weak. Like Donner Pass pioneers they overcame starvation with cannibalism, but queens won't lay eggs when their hives are so distressed, and bee numbers have sunk below those we originally hived. Even so, with the improved weather and fresh nectar sources, we're still hopeful that these hives are strong enough to store honey for their own winter use.

Loggers are far enough away over the hill to mask their noisy destruction, and except for bee hum and birdsong, the immediate world is calm and quiet. Views stretch for miles in every direction—only undulating green, and more green under an azure sky with not a single building, cell phone tower or road in sight.

I wander away from the yard and hike up a hill dotted with mauve, pink and white foxglove, pausing to watch a desperate honeybee disappear inside the hanging flower bell of a foxglove then quickly back out with tremendous difficulty, buzzing loudly. Foxglove nectar is poison to honeybees, leaving them drunk and disoriented. Perhaps the agitated honeybee is young and only now learns a lesson that foxglove isn't a nectar of choice. Plants choose their pollinators, and a nearby bumblebee, although larger than the honeybee, has no problem with the same maneuver, as he enters and exits a flower bell with ease. Bumblebees look like experts, despite their bumbling, especially with these foxgloves.

With the sun high overhead, shade is almost non-existent. I crouch at the base of a recently planted fir for the meager shadow offered by spindly boughs, but within seconds curse the sharp stems and thorns of last year's thistles and spiky new growth that blanket the ground and ruin my resting place. Then I remember the masses of sweet-scented blooming Canadian thistle that will soon blanket these hillsides, and thistle produces excellent honey. In future I'll try not to think unkind thoughts of a plant so generous with food for the bees.

But until the thistles bloom, the bees are hurting. They scavenge from scarce clover on logging roads, gather minimal nectar from wild raspberry blossoms and resort to drunken dalliance in foxglove thimbles. We have no expectations of a honey harvest from the Quilcene yard this year.

Before our downhill trip, we turn on the CB again. Logging trucks are headed uphill. Just as we pull over onto a platform, an empty monster roars past. The huge beast kicks up a choking dust cloud that settles over vegetation for twenty feet on either side of the road. The trucks are greedy for another load of trees. Rip 'em out, chop 'em down and load 'em up. Perhaps one day Earth will grow plants and animals unattractive for man to harvest. But then humans would no doubt find a way to kill those too. Herbicides and pesticides already do a good job. Not to mention concrete and global warming.

Back home by early evening, I carry an empty super to the kitchen hive. The bees are far happier than those at the Quilcene yard earlier today, and even before opening the hive I know from the blissfully sonorous hum that they've been active all day. A long night of honey fanning lies ahead. When I lift the hive lid, hundreds of inquisitive eyes peer up at me. Who is this intruder come to spy on their hard work? The bees scurry down the frames when I squirt a puff of smoke spray. I quickly position the new box on top of the hive and replace the lid. Happy fanning and honey moving, sweet girls, and goodnight!

Early morning. I check the hive again. Even though the sun hasn't yet peeked over the treetops, a large cluster of bees clings to the front of the hot hive body. Early fliers already come and go with golden bounty while workers line up at the entrance, busily fanning wings to take moisture out of the hive and dry the honey. Scout bees dance a 'waggle dance' around the entryway to share the location of the latest greatest patch of wildflower or garden blossom. Two steps forward, one step back, turn and turn and turn again: fly south ten yards, turn left, veer right to where seductive flowers flaunt scent and color, then gorge on ripe nectar.

Inside the top box placed on the hive yesterday, a shallow 'super' for honey storage, frames are still quiet, though I'm sure not for long. The heavy second box is full of bees, honey, brood and eggs. The bottom box is also heavy with bees, brood and eggs. This is one healthy hive.

Blackberries rush into bloom. More and more each day. Already the king bloom, the primary central flower, has blossomed and secondary flowers open further down the stems. The thorny plague won't be restrained, as it creeps effortlessly through the countryside and on to invade cities where it grabs hold along bike paths, overruns freeway slopes, sprouts in side road ditches, invades trails, obliterates neglected backyards and engulfs vacant city lots. Herbicide, leather glove, and machete industries do brisk business in the Pacific Northwest with its ideal climate for appetites of the ambitious berry-bearing creeper.

I've always loved blackberries for the berries, and never minded the picking hazards of scratches or torn clothes. And beekeepers especially love blackberries. Blackberry blossoms are the primary endless source of overflowing nectar at this time of year. We are prepared.

We deliver a truckload of supers to the 'eagle' bee yard near town where towering bushes of white blossom crowd hives like a wedding party around a wedding cake. The bees are working overtime–day shift, swing shift and graveyard–with top supers almost fully capped with fresh honey. Taking off the almost full supers, we place empty supers underneath, then replace the top box. This way, bees will fill the top box, honey will be ready to pull by the end of the week and the bees will still have space to store their goods. Honey labeled Blackberry/Wildflower tops the list of our market inventory.

Driving through a tunnel of green next to the Beard's Cove bee yard, the pickup brushes through leaf curtains that leave long drapes of nettles on the antenna and side mirrors. The entire landscape is overgrown. I stand under an eight-foot-high clump of grass with waving fat grain heads. Nearby, first small hard apples hang from abandoned homestead trees; red berry sprays entice birds to elderberry bushes. Globs of cuckoo spit, like whipped egg white, encase high grass stems. Dusty-pink steeplebush blossoms spire upward from a choking mass of ever growing summer vegetation.

At twilight, hives hum from field bees hard at work inside after an eighteen-hour day of thousands of successful nectar flights. Clusters of second-shift workaholics fan non-stop at hive entrances long into the night. Some bee skyscrapers now tower a formidable seven boxes high. Honey harvest is close.

"It's that time of year again," Roy announces triumphantly as he opens the door to the extracting room. Yesterday, while I sold at a market, he harvested the first honey of the season.

The small extracting room, behind the main workshop 'honey house', has space for two radial extractors, an uncapping sink and a wall lined with honey-filled boxes. Plus two people. The room is small and easy to heat. And, today, it is hot. Hot and sweet. As I enter the room the temperature blasts ninety-five degrees and I'm reminded of landing in Mumbai or Lagos and stepping into a land of overwhelming heat and smell. But the difference is that this smell is the sweetest freshest honey.

Except for having one's head inside a beehive, nothing can compare with the intoxicating scent of a honey extracting room. Bees maintain temperatures in a hive close to ninety-two degrees. Inside the extracting room, the slightly higher temperature helps honey flow freely from the frames.

My senses dissolve in the sweet olfactory feast and I could lose myself in a dream of exotic honeyed visions. But first to work, extracting the honey.

After bees have dried honey in frames to the right moisture level for storage, they cap and seal the honeycomb with a light coating of wax. The extracting process begins with scraping the wax capping from either side of the honey-filled frames with heated knives. The wax falls into the capping sink below and then any honey left in the capping wax drains through a mesh strainer into a bucket. Several of our customers, especially Eastern Europeans, treasure 'cappings honey', with its pieces of wax, occasional bee parts and a larva or two.

We uncap frame after frame by drawing our hot knives up under the top coating of wax, then open any missed capped cells with a spiked comb-like utensil. After uncapping each frame we insert them one by one into slots, like spokes of a wheel, inside each of the two cylindrical stainless steel extractors.

When all twenty slots are full, we set the machines to spin, slowly at first, then increase the speed faster and faster until honey flies out of the comb and slides down the metal walls to the spigot. Roy opens the tap over a five-gallon bucket and....*Voila!* Out pours the first liquid gold of the year.

The very first sample has a distinct maple flavor, reminiscent of maple syrup, from this spring's maple blossom. The dark gold honey slides smooth and rich over my tongue, with an initial burst of sweetness and a mellow maple aftertaste. Delighted with the promising start to the year's honey harvest, we can't stop grinning.

When all the honey has spun out of the frames, we empty the extractors and re-place the sticky dripping frames in the recently emptied boxes. These boxes are ready to be returned to the hives as soon as possible, where, attracted by the fresh honey scent, bees will rush to refill the sweet honeycomb.

Sweating and exhilarated by the taste of the season's first honey, we take a break in the cool evening outside the extractor room. Overhead, a dark sky twinkles with a million stars.

Back in the honey house, Roy pours buckets of fresh honey into the bottling tank. He opens the spigot. Golden amber liquid glides like melted butter from the tank into hexagonal honey jars. This early season honey combines nectars mostly collected from evergreen huckleberry blossoms, big leaf maple bloom and red vine maple flowers. I label the jars Huckleberry/Maple Honey.

CHAPTER 18

EARLY SUMMER FINDS

A SHAVED steel sky presses against treetops around the clearing and spits misty drizzle as I hike the river trail past the Guardian of the Forest. The Guardian serves us well. Our new neighbors keep a low profile and I no longer fear meeting them in the woods or by the river. But the shadowed woods feel gloomy and sullen and I long for sunlight to filter through the dense leaves. Where are the bright summer days of June?

On either side of the path, a second layer of forest mantle, shoulder high bracken, shadows undergrowth and the forest floor. At the beach I search for color. Tiny blue speedwells between beach pebbles add a touch. Maturing vine maple leaves begin the shift from luminous green to reddish orange with fully formed helicopter maple seeds already poised for take-off.

Then something bold and bright catches my eye. Here is my color. A cinnabar moth lands on a beach stone, the first time I have seen this stunning moth. Its black and blood red wings resemble dramatic wind surfing sails with triangular upper wings, black with a red border on two sides and red dots on the third. Lower wings are all red. The word cinnabar comes from the ancient Persian word 'jinjifrah' meaning dragon's blood. Mercury sulfide, the mineral used by alchemists to produce quicksilver, was named cinnabar for its color. I name the moth 'the Alchemist'. Cinnabar moths were introduced from Europe in the 1970s to combat tansy ragwort, a plant noxious to cattle. The adult moth lays her eggs on ragwort leaves, which the hatching orange/black tiger-striped caterpillars then devour. Fortunately the moth hasn't yet devoured every tansy leaf then changed forage patterns as some introduced species have when they've wiped out their host plants and then moved on to wreak havoc on other innocent vegetation.

On my hike home, my awareness heightened and alert after the moth sighting, two stems with unusual greenish heart-shaped flowers catch my attention. Each eight-inch stem has a pair of leaves; dainty flowers balloon at intervals on the top two inches. Without requesting the plant's permission, I stoop and pick a flower for identification. I immediately regret it. So much for my heightened awareness. The plant might be a rare species. I should have brought the field guide to the blossom.

I identify the plant as a tway blade orchid. Excited to find wild orchids on our land, I return with Roy to show off my exotic discovery, but searching everywhere, I'm unable to locate the plants as they hide from my greedy eye. Serves me right for picking without thinking. I'm relieved when, the next morning, I search again and the orchids reappear.

☼

Flashes of orange shine through high bushes by the driveway where wild honeysuckle vines twine like snakes along a fir branch. Blossoms dangling from bluish green leaf collars are as vibrant and spectacular as any tropical Hawaiian flower.

After hiking twenty yards on Tall Trees Trail I am in thick forest, alone, with no brush pickers to disturb my peace of mind. Leaving the trail to dive deeper into the trees I soon find an inviting throne of an overgrown cedar stump, sink onto a welcoming mossy cushion and lean back into the crumbling soft bark. Wind rushes and roars through upper forest branches drowning all other sounds, then the wind quiets. Bird calls and melodies filter through the woods. Twitters become the background soundscape, and then one song outdoes the others when a winter wren, even though it is summer, warbles a series of trills, quavers, and bubbling squeaks. I count more than five seconds of ecstatic song with each melodic repetition.

This morning's rain scarcely touched the forest floor, but drops etch shiny patches on dusty undergrowth beneath gaps in the thick canopy. Above me, only small fragments of overcast sky are visible. Where light puddles through to the forest floor, sword fern and bracken stretch toward the sun; where shadows fall, Oregon grape sprouts dusty berry clusters; completely shaded areas are home to scrubby moss. Vine maple leaves quake in the breeze beside swaying drapes of lichen.

Luminous fat raindrops begin to fall as I wander further down the trail, but I am well sheltered by these trees. To my left, crowds of giant fern clutch at a steep slope where the cliff edge drops suddenly to the marshy river valley. Nine-inch-long leaves of a large trillium plant hide under a fern frond beside the trail and I know that I want to be amazed by the size of this plant's bloom next year. But will the trillium still be here in the spring? I build a small twig cairn by the path so I can find the plant again, trying to make the marking inconspicuous but visible enough to trigger my memory.

Leaves and ferns rule. Today's forest flowers-of-the-moment, tiny sprays of foamflower and white star blossoms, twinkle shyly in the flow of never-ending green.

The wind picks up speed again, pushes and sways one-hundred-feet-tall trees; leaning firs scrape and creak like dungeon doors. Birds stop singing. Raindrops patter on big leaves as I attune my hearing to distinguish between slightest subtle sounds but cannot recognize the source of a faint intermittent grinding noise. Is it a bird, an animal, or a tree? Everything feels alive and slightly ominous. But when I listen intently, the forest isn't ominous. I only feel anxious when my mind flashes to thoughts of our human neighbors. Unseen wrens, other small birds and tiny creatures scurry, dart and rustle in the leafy undergrowth. A bumblebee zooms in and circles close, assessing who I am and why I'm here. In the background, the buzz of bumblebees crescendos through the forest as waves of sound crest and fall in rhythm with the rush of wind.

☼

Towers of blooming wild rhododendrons around a nearby beaver pond transform a somber forest into a fairy fantasy. Hoping for an idyllic photo, I stumble through brush and deadfall under blossom archways to find the best viewpoint. At the pond's edge, where last month I captured a flawless photo of dramatic tree reflections on motionless sunset water, I glance across to the opposite shore. To my disgust, a crumpled beer can on top of a stump at the water's edge mars the award winning scenery. My perfect picture trashed, I hike around the pond to remove the offensive litter.

My far too noisy steps snap twigs and branches. A great blue heron rises from mid–pond, magnificent and startling, and flies north. Time slows as she flaps her broad wingspan; her beak poised straight ahead, her s-curved neck tucked close to powerful shoulders.

I slow down. Once again I have to remind myself to be quieter and more aware when tromping through woods and around ponds. Too often I am rushed, inattentive and over-excited by my amateur explorations, thrilled by nature, angered by trash and anxious about leaving my car vulnerable to vandalism beside a seldom-used back-road.

The view from the far side of the pond is breathtaking. Along the shoreline, reeds shoot thick and straight from bright water; golden lily cups weave among lily pads beside the reeds. The water shivers with reflections of lavish blossom on a twenty-foot rhododendron bush while firs and leafy shrubs provide a dark backdrop to the flow of light and color.

The pond has all the beauty of Monet's garden at Giverny. But with a difference. Here there is nothing manmade, no gardener, no intentional planting. This natural wild garden confidently adds touches of dying branches, last year's dead rushes, weathered stumps and snags. Refusing to hide ongoing cycles of dissolution, nature wears her wrinkles with a smile.

☼

Two weeks later I revisit the same beaver pond. Water has receded around the shrinking pond, leaving a two-foot mud apron that reveals a grim legacy of trash. Again I am disgusted. And depressed. Visitors with no respect for natural beauty have left a trail of plastic, cans, tangled fishing line, diapers and paper through woods close to the pond's edge. Hurrying away through the trees to a less accessible corner of the lake, I hope for fewer traces of human carelessness.

Halfway through the forest, I stumble into a small clearing where there's a patch of disturbed earth. Someone has dug a hole and filled it in. Feeling uneasy, I stop at the edge of the clearing while my over-active imagination revels at the chance for speculative scary possibility. A shallow grave? Maybe, but the size is round and smaller than the length of a body. Maybe a dog. But why would somebody haul a dog so far into a hidden place in the forest? Someone has buried something that they do not want found. My initial response is: leave! Forget you even saw it! I hurry away, but my imagination won't let go of the mystery of what might lie hidden in that hole. Thoughts nag me to do something, however small. I should go to the police.

All night my mind restlessly returns to the hole in the woods, so first thing in the morning I pass along the information to the sheriff's office. Early in the evening I rendezvous with a deputy by a crossroads in the forest and he follows my car to where I park near the beaver pond. He grabs a shovel from the trunk of his patrol car and follows me around the pond and through the trees to where I found the dug-over earth. As we pass the pond, I pause to point out the dramatic beauty of evening tree shadows on the water. The deputy appreciates the view and comments that most people wouldn't even notice the picturesque scene. They obviously didn't, considering the amount of trash.

118

We hike to the suspicious clearing. I'm nervous as he pushes his shovel into the dirt. What if it is a body? A small child? Perhaps it *is* just a dog buried in the woods. But if it's a dog, why isn't there a small cross or at least a pile of stones? The deputy easily turns over a couple of shovelfuls of soft earth from the three-foot-wide depression. Then, eighteen inches below the surface he uncovers a black plastic bag, tightly knotted at the neck but ripped apart underneath. He lifts out the bag with the end of his shovel and shakes off the dirt. The bag is empty. He turns up two more plastic bags, both empty, knotted at the neck, ripped at the bottom. What was buried in the bags? Why are they open at the bottom? Did an animal scavenge the contents? Unlikely. Someone came and took the contents. Fast.

The Deputy keeps digging. The metal shovel smacks against metal in a fourth plastic bag. This one is not empty.

"Times like these I think I'm not paid enough," he mutters, then laughs, "at other times I think I'm paid too much." Lifting the last bag out of the hole, he gestures for me to move away.

I take a couple of steps back. I'm not taking a chance on an explosive. Several layers of black plastic have been tightly wound around a two-foot-long metal object. He pokes and prods at the bundle with his shovel and a stick (he has no gloves, and doesn't want to touch the 'evidence'). The metal barrel of a shotgun breaks through the plastic. The gun has been broken down into pieces.

Judging from the gun's wrapping we guess that whoever buried it plans to return. The shotgun must have either been stolen or used in a crime. We guess too that someone already returned to empty the other bags. Did they contain money? Drugs? Guns? These dark woods hold dark secrets.

The deputy pauses from digging and tries unsuccessfully to call his supervisor on his cell phone. We are so far in the forest that he cannot reach his supervisor but manages to contact a third party who can relay messages.

There is no reason for me to stay and I don't want to linger longer in this dismal place as night creeps between the melancholy trees. The Deputy thanks me for passing on the information about the suspicious hole. I leave him waiting for instructions whether to continue the excavation or leave the crime scene for a detective to investigate tomorrow. I hurry back to the road through the shadowy forest, glad to reach my car before complete darkness. I doubt that I will return to these woods alone any time soon, however idyllic the Giverny-like beaver pond and wild rhododendron blossom.

CHAPTER 19

SWARMS AND MOVING BEES

GOOD NEWS. The suspicious character in a trailer on the timber company's property at 'huckleberry heaven' is the brother of a logger working in nearby woods, and the man camps on the land in exchange for guarding previously vandalized logging machinery. We will move bees right away, glad there's nothing sinister to worry about and happy that acres of nearby huckleberry are in bloom.

The ideal time to move hives is either early morning before field bees leave the hive or late evening after they've delivered their last nectar load.

At 5:00 am Roy and Ian leave to pick up a load of hives from Beard's Cove. At 7:30 am the white truck rumbles and creaks back down the driveway, the flatbed weighed down by full boxes of bees ready to move to the site we call 'the pond'. After fixing a pancake breakfast (with huckleberry honey) I join them to set up the new yard.

The orange gate to the company land hangs open. Loggers are everywhere this summer. We witness more activity than most people when we drive up logging roads to leave hives on privately owned timberland. Companies often avoid cutting trees where the public can witness the results, leaving a token veil of trees along highways to disguise just how much forest has disappeared. But we know. If the companies disregard timber growth requirement limits, I guarantee that there won't be trees to cut, and the loggers' grandchildren, or even children, won't be receiving a paycheck from the timber industry.

Roy has already set up a bear fence in a clearing lined with huckleberry bushes and surrounded by acres of fireweed. He backs the truck inside the fenced perimeter of the yard and we unload the hives in record time. Working from the flatbed, Roy hoists hives onto the loader and slides them out along the boom. Ian catches the loader, swings the boxes into position and lowers them onto rows of pre-positioned wooden hive stands. He places taller, densely populated hives at the center of the rows, leaving shorter weaker ones on the outside. Bees tend to drift to outside boxes, so the outer, smaller hives will become stronger.

Around the yard, purple and white foxglove tower over the green and gray/brown undergrowth; orange tiger lilies dance above the salal; tangles of trailing blackberry with white blossom and ripening berry clusters crawl beside the road. If the weather cooperates, the bees will soon sail over surrounding trees to explore several acres of clear-cuts now turned wildflower meadows.

Once all the hives are in place, Ian runs up and down the rows removing entrance closures. The bees are free to explore. Hundreds pour like a fire drill from four or five hives, anxious to see where they are, curious to know what the jiggling and banging was about. But at other hives, the bees are cautious and only one or two girls crawl nervously into the light to view their changed world.

Roy drives the truck out of the yard and hooks up the electric fence. Now all we need is hot weather for fireweed beyond the trees to pump out water-white nectar.

At home, an unusually large mass of bees robs old hive boxes, and I suspect something to do with swarming. Perhaps the robbers are scouts searching for real estate to squat. Or, more likely, the bees are filling their bellies before a journey.

When I scan a tall fir near the kitchen hive, my instincts prove correct. Just call me swarm detective.

A swarm, larger than a football, sways from a branch about fifteen feet up in the fir. The bees cling to each other and, where twigs and branches make a perfect ball impossible, they form acrobatic bee-chains. The swarm must be from the kitchen hive, but when we look inside, the boisterous population and resonant hum appear healthy. The population exploded while we weren't paying attention. This season things happen fast and we've never seen as many hives swarm as this year.

We pull on bee suits and grab a ladder, hive tools, bee brush, saw and an empty hive box. Roy cuts away small branches under the swarm and climbs into the tree while I hold the ladder at a precarious angle. Balancing the empty hive box on one arm under the swaying ball, with his free hand, Roy yanks the branch above the swarm. A furry waterfall gushes into the frames. Several hundred more bees fly about in confusion. Roy retreats down the ladder with the box, replaces the lid and leaves the box under the tree. A river of bees flows over the landing board and pours into the hive entrance.

But the next day all the bees have left the hive and headed back to the fir branches. The queen must have felt at home on the limb, decided to stay, and the bees chose to rejoin her. Since the swarm is large, we will recapture the bees. And the queen. There is no future in a palace without royalty.

This time, Roy jerks the fir limbs fiercely until every last bee falls off the branch into a large cardboard box, then he empties the box into the waiting hive. Now he's certain that he corralled the queen, and we have the bonus of a second kitchen hive.

Roy doesn't always choose to capture swarms. Last week he received a call asking him to catch a swarm at the Theler wetlands, but because of its small size, decided not to chase the renegade bees. The swarm left for the woods. Everyone will benefit if these honeybees survive in the wild for pollination, plus someday they might surprise some worthy beekeeper by reoccupying an empty hive. Or maybe they'll shack up in a hole in a wall of someone's house, hopefully someone who enjoys bee-buzz, honey, and fascinating hours of watching dozens of industrious fuzzy insects.

Many hives at different yards are acting in a way that Roy has never seen in all his years of beekeeping. Some hives are collecting honey, building brood and staying busy just as they always do at this time of year, but other hives hustle to create supersedure cells for new queens and swarm whenever possible. It must be the Russian queens. They like to swarm.

Repeated swarming requires constant vigilance and extra work for a beekeeper trying to harvest a honey crop, but if a swarm does escape, the ecosystem reaps the rewards of valuable pollinators. Nature works hard for survival.

Working late into the luminous summer evening, we extract and bottle some of the smoothest honey I have ever tasted, mostly huckleberry, with a hint of maple and a myriad of other unidentifiable flavors. I've yet to emulate the extended tasting metaphors used by wine-tasting connoisseurs. Aromatic, fruited and mellow is a beginning. I set aside a quart jar for our own kitchen.

Brackish marsh, huge nettle stands, salmonberry bushes, horsetail and high-grown summer vegetation blend in a crock-pot of hot jungly smell as we drive through the leaf tunnel to the Beard's Cove bee yard.

Bees zing from all sides of the old homestead site in perfect honey weather. The yard is Grand Central station at rush hour, jammed like a Tokyo subway, frantic with weaving golden speedsters. With fifty-five hives in close proximity, and an average of sixty thousand bees per hive, that's about three million bees. Bees zip every direction in darting chaos. This would be an air traffic controller's nightmare, but not for these bees whose navigation skills are honed to perfection. I've never seen a mid-air bee collision. Some fly out diagonally, some fly up and swing a u-turn above a neighboring hive, while others circle and hover before speeding off for another sweet shipment of nectar. They leave the hives almost weightless, light and agile, and return fast, weighed down by a full heavy load.

Later, at home, another swarm swirls to the edge of the river slope, circles, and lands half way up a fir. We didn't see which hive it escaped from, but judging by the small size, the swarm must have left the same kitchen hive that swarmed only a few days ago. Since the swarm is so small, we let it escape with our blessing to fend for itself in the wild. I put my ear against the first kitchen hive and hear the high peep of queens. That means only one thing. Even more queens have hatched and now fight to the death. Soon there will be yet another swarm. We can't keep up!

CHAPTER 20

MOUNTAIN MIGRATION

EACH SUMMER we transport our hives to higher and higher and greener and greener, or in our case, pinker and pinker pasture. These summer journeys stir in me a deep resonance with migratory mountain traditions of nomads across the world, an instinctive bond with resilient herders of the Andes, Alps and Himalayas who, for centuries, have moved sheep, goats, cows and yaks in rhythm with the seasons.

As bee herders we take our livestock into the high country for long summer light and late blooming wildflowers, then bring them down to the protection of the lowlands for winter. We are wildflower chasers, searching for every opportunity for our bees to collect pollen and nectar away from polluted air, and as far as possible from pesticides and herbicides of twenty-first century agriculture, chemical lawn fanatics and backyard 'beauty' fiends. We want our honey to be as 'organic' as possible. In the Olympic Mountains our lucky bees fly on a clean summer breeze that blows from the Pacific Ocean with no cities for thousands of miles.

☼

Under hot late afternoon sun, Roy, Ian and I load bear fence equipment into the red pickup and leave to set up two new bee yards above Hoodsport.

The road winds along the south shore of the Hood Canal past idyllic sounding roads named Sunset View Lane, Pebble Beach Drive, Hummingbird Lane and Twanoh Tides Drive. Roadside banks pump out green, green and more green. Ditches overflow with shady blackberry, maple and alder, horsetail, ferns, wild sweet pea and daisies. Tree trunks are barely visible through thick fur coats of moss and ivy. Cedars and madrona lean at precarious angles above the Canal beach, only a matter of time before banks collapse in a winter storm and the trees become driftwood. Low tide water on the Canal shines like glass.

We cross onto the Skokomish Indian reservation. The delta of the Skokomish River (the 'Skoke') fans out in a fertile farmland flood plain, often under water in heavy winter rain. But today, in the heat of summer, the Skoke flows slow and mild. Reservation firework stands cluster at the corner of Highway 101: Pyromamas, Pyrokids, Mad Dog, Finish Line, Wind Talkers, Pink Cadillac, Good Fellas, Rez Skins, Match Box and Viper. The stands have closed for another season, soon to be dismantled until next year. We turn right onto Highway 101 and head north along the western shore of the Hood Canal through Potlatch to Hoodsport.

In Hoodsport we veer west toward the mountains, follow the winding road to Lake Cushman and at about 1,000 feet turn right onto a gated logging road that runs parallel to Highway 101 through State land. We have keys. Inside the gate, we again drive through a landscape rapidly being shorn of irreplaceable trees. Goodbye beautiful forests. On our journeys, Roy often announces "Another beautification project!" From close to our home on the Tahuya Peninsula we can look across the Canal to where we are now and see the spreading scars left by clear cuts, but somehow, from a distance, the hills don't appear as devastated, covered by a Band-Aid of fast growing low vegetation. Up close it is not so pretty. Hundreds of acres have been cleared since last year. I think I know why gates are locked, even though this is public State land. I suspect the State doesn't want the public to know the extent and speed of tree disappearance, although they tell us the reason for the locked gates is to protect valuable resources from fire and vandalism.

Crumpled brown alder leaves and dying thistles on either side of the road warn that herbicides were recently sprayed in the area. Good sense tells me it would be smarter for someone to cut vegetation with a brushwacker or mowing machine, but timber industry bottom lines show dollar savings with a truck spraying at twenty miles an hour, regardless of future costs to the environment. Fortunately the sprayed area lies more than two miles from the proposed bee yard site.

A detour is under construction for logging trucks to have faster, easier access to trees. The new road bypasses a narrow winding hill down to a creek and hairpin bends on the far side of the gully. Keep the old roads! Slow the trucks! Again, dollar figures and politics dictate who receives money for new roads instead of maintaining old ones. At least a thorny grove of devil's club in the gully will be saved by the diversion.

Despite my angst at the prevalence of habitat destruction, the hillsides and logged meadows are aflame with the beauty of bright fireweed, which the bees adore. Bunched heads of fragrant, pollen-laden pearly everlasting inch into bloom. Foxglove, daisy and rhododendron play a final encore of color, if not bee food, while St Johns Wort, ragweed and other yellow stragglers brighten the dusty undergrowth.

We stop to unlock another access gate. A slight movement rustles grasses to the south. It isn't the wind.

A bear! A black bear.

I leap out of the truck. My heart pounds. Camera in hand I grab a quick shot as the large animal ambles up a sloping scrubby meadow of tall grass, berry bushes and blooming fireweed. The mellow bear moves with lumbering ease toward a road that runs underneath power lines about twenty yards downwind. I am as excited, clumsy and fumbling as the bear is nonchalant, majestic and relaxed. He pays no attention to us, although he turns his head in our direction. With his poor eyesight he appears not to have seen us and rambles on through high grass toward the road. I crouch low and, under cover of bushes, scramble to the road above where he will cross. I wait for him to reappear.

Moments later the bear parts the grasses and lumbers onto the gravel, his flopping gait showing beginnings of stored winter fat. He pauses motionless under the power lines, sniffs and gazes solemn-faced in our direction. Magnificent, solid, lustrous, black and healthy, the muscular wild beast weighs five or six hundred pounds. My heart beating fast, I step onto the road in full sight of his turned head and take another picture of him under the power lines. Unperturbed and, after sensing nothing to fear from our direction, the bear saunters into bushes on the far side of the road either oblivious of our presence or just unconcerned on his daily reconnaissance of bear territory.

"Wow!"

"Awesome!"

"Amazing! What a beauty."

We are exuberant, in contrast to the mellow bear. I have never seen a bear this close in the wild. Neither have Roy or Ian.

"What would we have done if the bear had charged?" I ask.

"I grabbed a gun when I jumped from the pickup. But it wasn't loaded!" says Ian. "So I don't know."

"I would have instinctively known in the moment," adds Roy.

Probably the same for me. I could have moved closer for a better photo since I was upwind, but caution warned me to keep my distance, respect his privacy, and just enjoy watching a bear wandering so casually and openly in his natural habitat. They are shy creatures.

Later, looking at the photos, I'm amazed by how much of the road under the power lines he covers. He's a large bear.

When I share the bear photos with people at markets they, in turn, share tales of bear encounters. Excitement and awe echo through every tale. Reverence for bears runs deep in any culture close to nature, and Westerners, by early association with our cuddly teddy bear friends learn affection for the wild animal from a young age. I know I did.

We drive on to the new bee yard site and set up a bear fence in record time and trust that the 'tongue-to-electric-sardine-can trick' will give effective protection from the hulk of honey-and-larva-loving animal we just saw. How puny and insignificant the fence looks compared to the oversized bear!

We leave the gated State land, follow the shoreline of Lake Cushman, turn from the main tourist paved road and take a less traveled road north through Hood Canal State Forest. We pass Lilliwaup campground and Lilliwaup Creek, then turn west up a steep old logging road into the Olympic National Forest high country under Mount Jefferson.

Since last year, speed bumps (mounds of dirt) and drainage ditches (mini-valleys) have been dug at intervals across the road, to slow down ATVs, RVs, ORVs, SUVs, and another over Vs bent on tearing up wilderness hillsides. Our little pickup lurches clumsily over the bumps and dips and Roy wonders whether the long-bed boom truck will be able to maneuver the obstacles when loaded down with hives.

Narrow hairpin bends wind upward through deep draws filled with red-berried devil's club. As we climb higher, two-hundred-foot firs grow straight up from precipitous rocky slopes. Higher yet, shoulderless rock edges drop thousands of feet from the narrow one-lane road. After all my years of driving here with the bees I still avoid the stomach-churning view from the truck window.

Today's trip is a reconnaissance to clear debris from roads and check for washouts. Old logging stumps, dislodged from barren sandy-soiled hillsides by winter wind and rain, slide downhill and come to rest on ledges cut by mountain roads. We have pickaxes for landslides and a chainsaw for fallen trees. Football-size rocks are easy to kick out of the way, but one root stump blocking the road takes the strength of all three of us to roll out of the way and over the cliff edge. Other than that, the way is clear. Last winter was relatively mild, with no major storms or mudslides.

As the elevation increases, the clock rolls back to springtime again. Fireweed plants grow thick and green, with only a hint of future pink flowers, while lupine and kinnikinnick still bloom prettily. Indian paintbrush flashes red against yellow daisy flowers of the fleabane, aster and sunflower family.

The pickup bounces, lurches and creaks as we turn onto smaller and smaller and bumpier and bumpier old logging roads till we reach the platform where we kept bees last year. I climb out of the cab, excited to stretch and breathe the clean high altitude air as deeply as I can, always grateful for these journeys to the healing high wilderness.

At 4,000 ft, a spectacular view sweeps the Canal, the Sound and sunset pink Mount Rainier. Roy calls this panorama 'the view from my office'. But today the view is marred. Almost no wind or rain has cleared the dirty air during a long hot spell and a foggy haze blankets the Puget trough along the 1-5 corridor. Only aware of the poor air quality when I look across at the city from a distance, the increasing smog is shocking. A pall of grubby brown air creeps further and further from Seattle and Tacoma city limits to stretch from Everett to Olympia. Our own frequent trips to city markets do nothing to lessen pollution.

Vandals have struck, even though this ledge is remote, hidden away and barely accessible. Some thoughtless delinquent, between last October and now, repeatedly ran over and flattened the bear fence. We left the fence up last fall when, after moving our hives, roads were too treacherous after a snowfall for us to risk an icy mountain drive to clear the yard and dismantle the fence. Perhaps the vandalism happened this spring. Previously, this same bee yard was the target of gunfire. But we're willing to give the site one more chance, as this yard has been one of our best fireweed honey and pollen producers. Although ruins of the downed fence infer otherwise, maybe vandals have matured since last year.

While I sell at a market, Roy and Ian move hives to the bee yard close to Hoodsport where we saw the black bear. Two days later Roy and I return to check the hives.

Bees are immediately agitated when we arrive. They want to be left alone with the hypnotic scent of mountain wildflowers and a strong nectar flow. No more meddlesome people in white. No more potential robbers. Perhaps a nosy bear has been eyeing several thousand recent arrivals and their tasty larvae. As soon as we get out of the truck, a handful of guards zoom to attention and surround us. I jump back inside, roll up the window and put on my bee suit and veil inside the cab. Roy fields a couple of stings.

We quickly give the hives extra boxes, sandwiching the new boxes between the top box and brood boxes below. Bees will move up, fill and cap honey in the top box first.

With our work complete, we picnic on the quiet hillside miles from other humans, close to where the bear crossed the road last week. How lucky we are to dine in a 'gated' community, our own private wilderness where views stretch for miles and large wild animals roam free. There's no need for ownership, only a deeply satisfying feeling of safety and belonging in nature.

☼☼☼

CHAPTER 21

NEIGHBORS

I AM AFRAID to visit the river. But not because of cougars, bears or anything else in nature. I can feel the presence of the new neighbors in the river valley even though I haven't seen them, I don't want to run into them by chance and doubt they want to run into me either.

Quietly, over the last two months, several men and women, a mobile home, a travel trailer, a motor home, two cars and two pickups have moved into the small clearing near the front of the next-door wooded property. Plus a hot tub. From glimpses I get from the end of their driveway, all the dwellings, vehicles and people look weather worn, except for a late-model sporty white mustang. Characters and vehicles change often. Dense undergrowth and trees shield the clearing from the community access road and from our driveway. Overgrown woods behind the clearing, above the river valley and close to our home, could hide any imagined illegal activity.

About ten families live along our road, surrounded by State Forest, beyond cell phone or TV reception, with the closest town, Belfair, nine miles away. We choose the privacy of hidden-away lives. Even though we are a small community, each family keeps to themselves, with minimal socializing except for a yearly road maintenance meeting, but the new neighbors have changed that. People now stop and talk on the road. But the community doesn't talk with the new neighbors. Only about them.

We suspect that they're a gang of identity thieves.

Last week one of Sharon's grandsons, from the ranch opposite the newcomers, told her he saw a woman rifle through our mailboxes and take mail. Last weekend, Sharon found a second-floor window screen slit open. Someone had climbed onto her porch roof and broken in while they were away for the evening. Nothing was visibly missing. The next day a sack of letters and packages addressed to a nearby scout camp disappeared from beside mailboxes at the end of the access road. Roy didn't receive last month's credit card bill. Unlocked country mailboxes are easy pickings for identity thieves.

The Sheriff and Post Office have been notified, but they say they can do nothing without evidence, and they won't listen to the word of an eight-year-old witness. Two weeks ago three garbage bags full of mail were found dumped in woods ten miles north of here.

The neighbors know they're suspected of mail theft. Last weekend an angry woman, who lives further down the road, blocked the neighbor's driveway while writing down license plate numbers. The confrontation soon spiraled into a violent shouting match.

I stay away from involvement in the conflict, relieved that my mail is delivered to a PO Box in town. I don't want to be sucked into the emotional 'us against them' community mentality and the steady escalation of accusations.

The peaceful neighborhood is splintering. Everyone is uneasy. I do not want to meet my neighbors in the woods.

☼

Another neighbor's new credit card is missing from his mailbox and the card has been used. The cardholder calls the Sheriff's office. The Sheriff tells him the Post Office must contact the

FBI. He calls the Post Office. The Post Office insists that the Sheriff's office must contact the FBI.

The time has come for someone to act as peacekeeper. We don't want to live in fear, scared in the woods, upset and uptight from paranoia spawned by the suspicious activity of newcomers. Roy decides that he must meet the neighbors and start a conversation to find out who they are and what they are doing.

Uneasy with him risking a potentially dangerous encounter, I watch as he confidently leaves our land well prepared with a steely bulge under his jacket. Another equally well prepared neighbor watches from a cover of bushes at the end of the neighbors' property.

Roy strides down the neighbors' driveway and knocks on the front door of the mobile home. No answer. He knocks again. A sleepy-eyed woman opens the door, steps onto the porch and quickly closes the door behind her. Roy hands her a jar of honey.

"Hi, I'm Roy, the beekeeper from next door. Welcome to the neighborhood. On behalf of the community you're warmly welcome to a great neighborhood if everything you're doing is legal and above board. But if it's not, well, the community won't tolerate criminal activity." He pauses, looks her straight in the eyes and adds, "There's some redneck mafia live in the neighborhood 'round here might outdo the meanest Sicilian mafia if you screw with them...."

The woman flinches. "I've done nothing wrong. It's my brother just released from jail and his girlfriend been causing trouble, they don't have any place to go. I let them stay in the travel trailer. I've asked them to leave. They won't be coming back."

She's nervous. Is she lying? Is she personally involved in criminal activity? Roy gives her the benefit of the doubt, always willing to see the best in people. He gives her a hug and leaves.

Roy is a brave man. Getting to know one's neighbors however briefly, with a visit, a jar of honey and a hug is a good overture to peacekeeping. Especially if the neighbors may be criminals.

Gunshots crack in the distance. Target practice.

Roy takes me to a secluded forest clearing and hands me a small pistol. I do not like guns. I am nervous and have never felt comfortable around firearms. Growing up in England, where gun ownership was illegal, at that time not even the police carried guns. As I take the pistol in my hand and aim at a paper target the hard steel of the gun feels alien, cold, heavy and ominous. The thought of actually having to fire at anyone seems unimaginable. Now, however, I do feel more secure knowing how to use the pistol, especially when I hike in these unfriendly woods in the shadow of our new neighbors, though I doubt that I'll wear the cold metal often.

I find a small handmade bent metal tool near where we park our vehicles and pick up the tool thinking that it belongs to Roy or Ian. It doesn't. It looks suspicious, the size and shape of the tool just right to pry out screens, open doors and jimmy open tough places. We think, but don't want to believe, that the tool belongs to our neighbors.

Roy takes the tool to town and shows it to the Sheriff's office, where a deputy suggests it might be a tool for adjusting brakes. Both Roy and I have had vehicles worked on at different shops in the last two weeks, so that is a possibility. We take the tool to the auto shops, but no mechanic at either shop recognizes or claims it.

Why was the tool on our driveway? We won't ask the neighbors if they own it. Even if we did ask, chances are zero that they would claim the suspicious tool. We guess that it may have been left as a warning calling card. They know we suspect that they're involved in illegal activity and maybe this is their way to scare us.

Two days later children from the horse ranch find a large open hunting knife under the mailboxes. Again, why was the knife left there? An escalation on the warning theme of the tool in the driveway? Insidious fear begins to weave a web of suspicion and low-level stress through the neighborhood. The secretive newcomers leave us very unfriendly messages despite Roy's friendly overtures. Why? If they are trying to antagonize us, they're succeeding.

☼

Sharon has watched the neighbors carrying paint cans, driving to town to buy propane, constantly loading and unloading plastic bins from vehicles and washing out the trunk of a car. Now we ask ourselves the obvious question. Are they making meth?

Byproducts and residue of meth manufacture are extremely toxic. Chemicals poured down a sink can quickly filter into the drain field then soak through the soil to ground water. Ten families have wells. We are the closest neighbors. Our well is only seventy-five feet from one of their trailers. Now I am angry.

What can we do? How can we find out for sure if they manufacture drugs or dump chemicals? No one wants to confront and question the neighbors directly, not even Roy. It doesn't take a PhD to know that we are not welcome to visit their homes or land.

Roy visits the sheriff's office in Shelton, the county seat. They reassure him that they will send someone to check the property for suspicious activity, then tell him that the county has meth labs all over the map. Profits are huge. Meth manufacture is fast easy money for maintenance of a drug habit with an enormous toll of addiction, crime, death and unusable trashed properties. Emergency rooms, courts and jails overflow with the tragic results.

Prohibition liquor stills and occasional marihuana crops seem benign compared to these chemical cocktail factories. Our woodland paradise has the potential to turn into a nightmare. No wonder the woods sometimes feel dark and sad this summer.

☼

137

Last night, gunshots jolted a peaceful evening. Then sirens. Roy hadn't returned from beekeeping. I locked the door and closed the curtains. Zap barked for half an hour.

An underlying edge of unease leaks into a gorgeous late summer day. The previously protective thick bushes and trees around our clearing now feel threatening. Neighbors could watch my movements from a number of places without being seen. And even if they have no interest in us whatsoever, their creepy vibes are difficult to ignore.

Two days later someone frees a stallion from his stall at the horse ranch while Sharon is away. They leave the stallion in a field with two mares, one of them in heat. Of course our neighbors are the usual suspects.

As we wind slowly up the twisting mountain road to Olympic bee yards we pull over by a draw filled with devil's club, a plant I've been attracted to recently. The plant's scientific name, Oplopanax horridus, literally means heavily armed horrid cure-all.

Armed from root to tip by vicious spikes and thorns, the plant was the bane of early loggers and settlers who struggled to clear land. For these pioneers, a tall stand of devil's club presented a hellish barrier of barbed weaponry. But Native Americans honored the plant, a relative of ginseng, and used it extensively for medicinal purposes, chopping and powdering the roots and inner bark to treat arthritis, ulcers, diabetes and digestive ailments. Tribes carved sticks into protective charms and fishing lures, burned the bark and daubed devil's club ashes and charcoal on their faces before ritual dances, believing in the power of the ashen masks to ward off evil influences, which gave the plant the reputation of strong protective medicine.

With our neighborhood situation, the timing is perfect for me to learn about a plant ally with strong protective powers and, even though I'm not ready to take the ashen-mask route, I am willing to test the plant's shielding properties for warding off negative forces.

Cautiously I reach out from the steep bank with a long stick and hook a length of spiked stem, very careful not to lose balance and tumble into the horrible barbed wilderness. The ten-inch piece of stem will serve as psychic protection for our home. Roy has a back up plan for more practical protection.

CHAPTER 22

River Memorial

DESPITE RECENT paranoia spilling into the community, I pluck up courage and pay a cautious visit to the river. Just call me a river junkie who must have her frequent river fix. Maybe I crave the river like the neighbors crave meth. Or maybe I just need the solace of fresh flowing water.

Everything is quiet. In dark woods by the river trail, glowing ghostly and luminescent, small groups of white Indian pipe have shot higher, about eight inches above the leaf mold. Ragged purple asters dance like street urchins between beach rocks. After minimal rainfall this month the river has shrunk, leaving side ponds and usual mud-filled hollows mere shallow craters sprouting fresh grass. A kingfisher swoops along the river course above my head and flies off downstream, his long fish-picking beak leading the way like the nose of a fighter plane.

The peace of the valley seeps into me, my river craving soon satisfied.

At the beach I slide my feet into the cool flowing water and wade upstream toward beaver ponds to the north, away from the land of bothersome neighbors.

A fast current pushes taut against my calves like a wrestler straining to push his partner off balance. Looking down through the rush of water to quivering riverbed pebbles for a hint of a safe footfall doesn't help. Plowing bravely through the racing water along the slippery riverbed, I defy the slimy round rocks with each treacherous step. My feet must sense their underwater path for themselves and I only trust my weight to them after they stop slipping as each foot slides to safe anchorage, firmly wedged between the slick stones.

Everything on the riverbed wavers with the distortion of carnival mirrors, and I realize how warped my view is when I catch sight of a handsome turquoise stone, plunge my hand to the bed and lift the stone to the daylight, to find that I hold in my palm a dull gray rock.

No wonder water equals the shifting medium of emotion. Too much and I fight to hold my balance against the flood. Too fast and I slip and slide and wobble with fear of being swept away. When my mind peers too deeply into the depths I risk being tricked by garbled interpretation and the false importance of my revelation. Water laughs at my perceptions. I wonder if I am becoming overly paranoid about the neighbors, swayed by the dramatic sentiments of the community. I feel powerless to suggest a way I can help ease the growing tension. De-fusing the antagonism and destructive activities of the suspected offenders feels far beyond my level of courage or ability.

I pause mid-river to gaze upstream, where deep-water pools under riverbanks reflect dark tree shadows. Beyond the tree shadows, tall grass reflections ripple in streamers over an eddy while the central current shimmers with mirrored clouds and blue sky. I reflect on how my own shadow appears when I least expect it, and how paradise always has a darker side in the endless cycle of creation, preservation and dissolution.

In quieter water I listen to the gentle slosh, splash and slurp a human makes when river walking. As I wade up the side stream to the beaver ponds, coyote, deer and raccoon tracks on the riverbank, beaver slips, and bear markings on an alder tree, let me know I am not alone. The other-than-human world in the valley is alive and well.

Water at the beaver ponds flows higher and quieter than earlier this year, trickling all around, but with less urgency. The rush of early summer has eased into the relaxed fullness of late July. Beaver have worked overtime to maintain the high water levels needed to protect their lodge entrance and full-time summer projects of layered stick and mud dams are almost complete. Construction sites are littered with piles of stripped bark, chewed through trees and ragged branches. One alder trunk, almost a foot around, is a felling-work in progress, embedded with toothy prints, a pile of wood chips underneath, and the tree above ready to topple.

Reeds and rushes clog channels; thorn bushes and brambles wield long spiky limbs; fallen tree branches become a challenging obstacle course. Going becomes slow and arduous, not the carefree meander of late May. But as I slosh through murk and oozing silt of muddy-bottomed beaver canals I remind myself that I don't live in latitudes where water moccasin, crocodile, leach and other dangerous creatures make river wading completely uninviting. There's already enough danger in the vicinity.

News arrives of the death of an old friend, Jimmy, a rare gentle nature spirit, a gardener and weaver who lived most of his too-short life in the mountains of Idaho. To ease my sadness, honor his memory and say goodbye, I create a simple ceremony to wish his soul safe journey to the other side.

Wind chimes by the woodshed clink on a light breeze.

With slow meditative movements I fill my harvest basket with blossoms of thirty-three garden and wild flowers: white clover, pink clover, red clover; white yarrow, red yarrow; golden California poppy, pink Icelandic poppy; wild aster and Shasta daisy; red bee balm and yellow marigolds; flowers from sage, dill, marjoram, parsley, oregano, rue, echinacea; bright fire engine red flowers of scarlet runner beans; a blue bachelor button; anise hyssop and St. Johns wort; white pea flower, radish flowers and a giant yellow squash blossom; hawkweed, vetch, wild violets, fireweed, white foam flower, hardtack, sweet smelling Canadian thistle and pearly everlasting. How Jimmy would have loved the scent and color!

With the overflowing basket over my arm, a cornucopia of texture, color and smell, I hike down to the river and wade to a fallen alder trunk below small rapids. I settle onto the sun-warmed log, feet dangling in the cool river-flow, the basket balanced beside me on the weathered wood.

Perched in branches of a nearby hemlock, a band-tailed pigeon coos a mourning dove song, huh whoo, huh whoo, huh whoo. A soft solemn requiem for a gentle soul.

Riverbank vine maples transition to fall red in a crossing of seasons. An orange and brown butterfly flutters into sight, dances in front of my eyes, swoops off along the beach and vanishes. How briefly life appears and disappears: the turning of seasons; the flight of a butterfly; the passing of a friend. Transformation and letting go.

My fingers dip into the fragrant basket and scoop out the rainbow of colors. One by one I toss petals and flower heads into the current with the whispered words "for Jimmy". Tender-eyed, I watch the blossoms float away, swivel and bobble from side to side on the curve of the river. Gold, pink, blue, white and crimson petals wash ashore on gentle sloped cobble beaches; bright flower heads catch in eddies, swirl and capsize, twirl and bump into fallen branches, then bob gleefully to the next snag. Purple-spoked echinacea glide and drift downstream. Cargos of splashed droplets sparkle in rose-petal boats. Water sucks, entices heavier blossoms to whirl downstream underwater through the deeper currents of river world.

Little fishes dart to nibble at the dazzle of rainbow gifts showering on the surface. A curious kingfisher swoops low to scrutinize the drifting festival. I free a feather trapped between river rocks, releasing it to float downstream with the flotilla of petals, visualizing its colorful voyage through the forest to woodlands, bobbing down the winding river past open fields to the estuary, to the Hood Canal, and out to the ocean.

I whisper a prayer for the return of Jimmy's soul to the source. Gateh, gateh, parasamgateh, bodhi svaha. Gone, gone, gone beyond, gone altogether beyond, what an awakening!

☼

Two weeks have passed since I visited the river. At first glance little has changed except that water runs slower and lower with more rocks visible on the beach. August has been unusually dry, with no rainfall forecast in the near future, but shady trees and moisture from the stream keep the valley green, and brave new leaves poke through beach pebbles. Late summer draws out warm days of slow transformation.

Lazy tree reflections quiver across the river. In a side pond, stringy green gunk clogs the stagnant low water, slimy and noxious. A hawk feather floats on the surface, slightly greenish from the slime. I bend down, pick up the feather, carry it to the main river to dabble in fresh water to clean it, then realize I may have done the wrong thing by aiding the spread of the jellied green gunk.

Flower heads clutch last petals before going to seed. Silky thistledown parachutes twirl and float above glassy water; maple leaves burn red against the bluest of blue skies; yellowed alder leaves bob downstream. Summer loosens grip of her opulent rule, although river's edge stands of bracken, reeds and brambles, green beyond their time, keep pushing against the inevitability of fall.

Plants that died back in the heat of summer have returned for a second act. Foxglove and baby alder send up new growth and stands of Cooley's hedge nettle sprout fresh pink bloom. Tansy, pruned earlier this year by armies of tiger-striped of cinnabar moth caterpillars, puts in a bid for another round. With not a single caterpillar in sight, tansy triumphs. At the water's edge pink bunched smartweed twines with yellow-trumpeted musk flower.

Beavers have been diligent. A blanket of willow leaves stripped from newly chewed branches floats on a backwater pool. Stringy green scum invades yet another pool and something that looks like dirty motor oil splatters leaves beside the river path. What is it? Has someone thrown toxic waste into the bushes? Neighbors? I am becoming paranoid. Roy tells me later the drips are a protective secretion produced this time of year by the trees.

I wander, receptive and open for revelation of a unique gift. And there it is! On the river, thirty feet above the logjam, a strange string-like phenomenon crosses the surface of the water. At first, it resembles fishing line, or a spider's thread stretched from one side of the river to the other, lying on the surface with its shadow dancing through clear waters onto riverbed rocks below. I grab a stick and try to lift the thread, but there's nothing there. I keep trying to move it, but there's nothing to move. A distinct line reaches across the river, a nearly invisible crack, drifting with the flow of water. It appears to be an almost transparent wall that water passes through, leaving behind a shadowed line. The line is not a branch reflection, which would cast a jagged shadow, but a break in the water moving slightly with the flow. I have never seen anything like it before.

The next morning I hurry to the river to see if yesterday's 'crack in the water' still exists. The line is visible, but closer to the logjam. I insist that Roy comes to see the phenomenon. Perhaps he has an explanation. He does. Water in a deep pool immediately behind the logjam is relatively stagnant. Water from the main current creates a conflict between moving and stationary liquid as it tries to enter the stagnant pool, and where the two fluids collide, the tension gives the illusion of a wall. Roy studied laminar and turbulent flow and has seen the phenomenon before.

☼

A phone call warns us of a suspected cougar somewhere along the river bottom. A German shepherd belonging to an upstream neighbor limped home at three in the morning with skin peeled

145

from his hind leg. Zap has barked sporadically at dusk for several days. But it is unlikely that the culprit is a cougar, for a large cat will lunge for the throat of its prey, not the leg. We've seen fresh bear markings on trees, so the attacker could have been a bear wandering close to the river.

CHAPTER 23

OLYMPIC BEES

BEFORE DAWN, we leave to move a load of hives from 'the pond' bee yard where the bees aren't doing well. At the yard, even though acres of fireweed grow nearby, the bees are lethargic and slow to bring in nectar. We had hoped that the bees would fly beyond the tall trees that surround the hives, but with almost no open view, and no flowers blooming immediately around the yard, the bees are depressed. Not good bee yard feng shui. Today we'll move the bees into the Olympics high above Hoodsport for the far healthier benefits of full sunshine, long hours of daylight, fine views, and acres of pollen and nectar bearing wildflowers.

At dusk yesterday we fastened bands around the boxes of each hive. Now, before sunrise, we place wire mesh screen closures in the hive entrances before field bees begin their eternal quest for forage.

Poking one closure too far inside an entrance with my hive tool, I carelessly bend the screen, leaving a small hole. A column of bees streams out. Not a good sign for the day ahead. Angry at their unexpected entrapment, they won't be recaptured. Meanwhile, some escaped bees reconsider their newfound freedom and crawl up and down boxes, desperately searching for a crack or hole through which to crawl back into their home. But we don't want to re-open the hive and risk losing even more bees, so we set up an empty single box with frames where stragglers and escaped bees can find shelter after we've left.

One by one we swing the hives onto the truck bed with the boom, then strap down the rows. By the time it's fully daylight we're ready to roll with a full load of hived bees and a hundred or so hitchhikers.

We drive cautiously around the south shore of the Hood Canal to the Olympics, stopping briefly at the Hoodsport Ranger station to let them know we're going to set up our new bee yards, for which we already have permits. A little cloud of a hundred or so escaped bees fly around the parked truck, still trying to figure out how to re-enter the hives. As soon as we move again, the bees ball up snugly between the hive bodies. Or so we think.

Hot sun rises above the mist as we grind out of the morning low fog into the mountains above Lake Cushman. The 'speed bumps' are effective. The long flatbed overhang scrapes across every bump as we lurch uphill, each time bringing us almost to a standstill. As the truck chugs up the steep incline in lowest gear, heavily weighed down by the full hives, we enter the dreamlike slow motion of a timeless journey, now and then stopping to check how far our honeybees have flown from hives already on the mountain. We watch Roy's girls enamored by purple pea vine, fireweed and ocean spray that grow almost two miles (as the bee flies) from the yard. Twists and turns of the logging road extend our own mileage considerably further than two miles.

After what seems like hours, at the bee yard platform, we look out across the Hood Canal and the Puget Sound, the latter still shrouded in a thick veil of mist. Behind us, Mount Washington, her stern dark face daubed with dirty snow, guards wide evergreen valleys and sheer Olympic mountain slopes.

We unload the hives as fast as we can, with great care to avoid upsetting the bees, but despite our concern, when I pull away entrance closures, bees rush out. They are pissed. Enraged. Hot. Slathered in alarm pheromones. I've never seen crowds of bees so eager to leave their hives. Trapped in overheated boxes for far too long as we climbed the mountain, they endured more bumping and rocking than their sensitive natures could stand.

By the time I approach the fifth hive to free the bees, an army crashes against my veil with screaming loud buzz. This is not the lazy murmuring drone of bees in the garden on a flowery summer's day. This is not the gentle hum of mellow golden pollen bearers. This is war. These bees are a murderous gang of escaped convicts intent on retaliation against their jailer.

The intensity overwhelms me. I leave the hives and walk out of the yard, trying to breathe deeply and stay calm. Roy takes over freeing the bees but, soon, he too is chased away. I find a fir tree and roll around in aromatic branches to disguise my scent. Roy disappears in the opposite direction. After a five quiet minutes, I step out from my cover of fir boughs thinking the bees have returned to their hives, but a dozen angry warriors zoom back and dive-bomb the thin netting of my veil again and again. I stride a hundred yards further up the road. Armed attackers and the heat batter my defenses, and even though I know I'm well protected inside my bee suit and veil, the high decibel onslaught is almost unbearable.

I find a shady outcropping of rock to lie back against and eventually, one by one, the hot bees leave me alone knowing they've succeeded in chasing me away from their domain. The air quiets. My attention spreads wide in the silence and I soak in a delicious moment of relative peace. Two crickets click lazily past and land on hot rocks.

Walking still further up the road, not yet ready to return to a war zone, I come to a small rock cairn and crudely etched concrete headstone leaning against a tree stump by the roadside. The simple memorial overlooks a steep drop to the Hood Canal with a view stretching uninterrupted for hundreds of miles of forest, mountain, water and sky. The headstone reads Dave Bayson, 1980-1998. Only a teenager. Is this is where the teenager's life ended? Was it one of his favorite places to visit? Or did his parents choose this place of wild beauty for remembrance?

Calmed by the memorial, I return to the bee yard ledge, but when I approach the truck, stubborn bees again hurl themselves at my veil. They know my scent. Regardless of peaceful thoughts I send them, I cannot convince them that I mean no harm. I give up and walk down the track away from the yard.

Roy finishes opening the hive entrances and suggests that we leave and return later when the bees have cooled off. Then we'll unband the boxes and crack open lids for better hive ventilation. Slowly retreating from the aggravated bees, we wait to take off our veils and claustrophobic bee suits until we're a hundred yards from the site.

Further up the mountain, weatherworn trees offer a welcome shady cover for a roadside picnic away from pissed-off honeybees.

Above us, a lightning-struck fir has lost half its upper trunk but courageously grown back another full tree off to one side. Nature heals itself the best it can. But nature cannot compete with the saw. Although these second growth trees are large, stumps on the slopes tell stories of much larger trees, giants by today's standards. How amazing this mountainside must have been little over a hundred years ago when a team of men sweated all day to cut just one tree. Today's rate of tree harvest is horrific. We're lucky to still have this shady picnic spot.

The forest echoes with the thwop, thwop, thwop of grouse somewhere close. Acres of wildflowers spread over hillsides. Some I recognize and can name: small white flowered hawkweed, pink wintergreen, mauve woodland penstemon, purple pea vine, light blue Scouler's harebell, orange tiger lilies, pearly everlasting and a broad splash of fireweed.

Every insect today is active and aggressive in the heat. Not only honeybees. Unprotected, away from the bee yard, we're again targets of aerial acupuncture as we eat our sandwiches. Waving, swatting and constant vigilance are not enough to prevent the onslaught of deer flies and other guerilla bugs. Regular flies and bumblebees are merely annoying.

Earlier this week, Roy hiked this slope looking for bee yard sites and found a promising location surrounded by heavy fireweed stands, but fallen trees blocked the access road. Today, a chainsaw and brushwacker clear the fallen debris fast.

The new site, our highest elevation bee yard, was once a logging truck turnaround on top of a steep hill with a scenic overview across the Sound even more spectacular than any so far. Remains of a fire pit, a disintegrating moldy foam rubber mattress, the usual beer cans, plastic bottles and shot gun shells litter the ground. Hundreds of bullet casings and shells scatter surrounding mountain slopes. When returning campers find a bee yard instead of a tent site, will their disappointment spawn revenge on our hives? Hopefully not.

We drive back to the angry bees at the yard below. Chaos reigns. The air is thick with buzzing, swirling, darting insects and hive fronts are black with massing bees. As soon as we pull up, guards fling themselves against the windshield. They remember their oppressors in the big white flatbed. I opt to stay inside the cab with the windows rolled up tight, unable to handle any more insect agitation.

Inside the truck the heat is stifling and close to 110 degrees as the sun bakes down through the glass. Starting to sweat in the cab sauna, I'm not about to open a window or door. But the temperature intensifies fiercely to an unbearable equatorial hot, and as soon as I think the coast is clear and don't hear buzzing or see bees, I dare to crack a window. Instantly an angry mob zooms up, searching for the opening. It's all about smell, and they're onto my scent like mice after cheese. I am prey. I immediately close the cracks. Sweat trickles over my eyebrows as I choose sweat over suicidal stings.

Much relieved when Roy finishes unbanding and ventilating the hives, we take off down the mountain with a welcome breeze flowing through the open window. We won't return to this site for several days while the bees adjust to the altitude, settle, explore, and tap into local food sources. Plus restore a considerably sweeter side to their disposition.

Without a load of bees, the truck bounces down the rocky mountain road. Fairy pilots, delicate fritillary butterflies, swoop and flutter downhill from flower to flower alongside and ahead of us, sometimes alone, sometimes in groups of two or three, chasing each other in a playful dance. At least some insects are not threatening.

At Lilliwaup campground, where Lilliwaup Creek lazes through the forest, we pull over under the shade of big leaf maples. I cross to a small island in the clear mountain creek, lie down on a bed of moss and sink my arms into the cold trickling water to soothe the swollen itch and heat of deer fly bites. Heaven! After a day of being targeted by hot flying bugs, my stressed nervous system relaxes into the cool green elixir of forest scent and stream. At waterline, an oak brown slug clings to a maple trunk draped with licorice fern. This slug is cool, soft, wet, vulnerable and slow, nothing like today's previous creatures. Slowly, the ripple of flowing water dissolves rough-edged memories of heat and buzz.

Back in Hoodsport, we stop briefly again at the Ranger station. When I open the truck door, a dozen honeybees appear from nowhere, waltz into the cab and hover around outside. These bees are not at all bad tempered, just curious to know where their hives have disappeared to. They must be hitchhikers who were hanging around outside the hives when we stopped here earlier, then zipped off to explore local flora and failed to return before we left. Now they smell the scent of their sisters, but where are their homes? Perhaps a local beekeeper has a hive ready to adopt these adventurers. Unless they opt to hitchhike home with us.

CHAPTER 24

Lazy Days

THE USUAL towhee sings his greeting wheeze. With old grandfather presence he surveys the clearing, day in, day out, calling for hour after hour from hidden leafy places behind the chicken coop. His soulful call is the first sound of morning and often the last sound of evening. At this time of year, his sentinel song stretches endlessly, and somewhat monotonously, from dawn to dusk.

I pioneer an alley to the river trail through wicked six-foot thistles. Spiky limbs thrust and grab my clothes. Clenched-fist purple flower heads rise up strong and united like a crowd of thorny revolutionaries, but these protesters merely intend to burst into intoxicating thistle fragrance.

At the river, light shimmers on pristine water. As I near the beach, two strident crows lift off and flap to the far bank calling that a human approaches. Bearers of news, views, gossips and cautions, the dark crows shout the latest bulletin like an old fire engine siren. Every bird, creature, insect and plant in the vicinity now knows of my presence, if they haven't already heard my less than stealthy step. The woods are on alert.

In sharp contrast to the noisy crows, a band tailed pigeon coos softly from a snag. The pigeon's repetitive melody resonates dreamy as a mystic lullaby through a drifting fog bank. No wonder her distant relative, the dove, is a symbol of peace.

Leggy St. Johns Wort shoots up from between beach pebbles. Just by gazing at the golden flower heads I instinctively know the uplifting healing powers of the bright scraggly plants. Close to the cool water's edge I pluck a sprig of wild mint, rub and crumble the leaves between my palms, cover my face with my hands and inhale deeply. A cooling burst of lightness zings through my senses. Perhaps if we honored, praised, and just sat with the healing smells, colors and feel of plants for five minutes every day, our medical bills might diminish considerably: immersion in nature as an alternative to expensive health insurance. Maybe office buildings should have herb gardens in their atriums.

Wading across a shallow stretch of river, stream water over my bare feet is as refreshing as the lingering cool scent of wild mint. At a small sandy beach on the opposite shore I feast on orange berries of full-fruited salmonberry bushes that overhang the bank, careful to avoid bitter overripe dark red berries. A cinnabar moth, the red and black alchemist, floats into view, settles on a tansy leaf, then beckons me up a dry creek bed through a break in the tangled bushes.

I hike away from the river into unexplored territory. How willingly I am led to the unknown in nature! A hidden bird repeats a melody that I try, unsuccessfully, to memorize for later identification: thweep, thweep, trill, tw, tw, tw, tw, rrrr. Another bird offers a steady rhythmic dweep, dweep, dweep, beginning low and rising higher. Birds thrill me with songs in the thick woods but I seldom see them, and although my ears invite their melodies, the sounds don't help identify the source from field guide photos. Not tempted to name, I sink deeper into an aural world of wonder.

A fallen cottonwood, reduced to a mossy, decaying trunk, sticks out of the beach at a forty-five degree angle. Under the trunk, a discarded pile of chipped bark and sawdust forms a small pyramid where a woodpecker has excavated a grubby feast. In shallow water, cut off from the main river, baby salmon squiggle restlessly, unaware that they won't survive if the pool dries up; for their sake I hope rain will replenish the water level long before the pool rejoins the river in fall.

Flowers have blossomed, faded and fallen. A handful of wild rose petals flutter on leafy bushes and already small rose hips bulge reddish along stems. Two kinds of huckleberry share root source on the same mossy stump: one dangles red waxy berries; the other, shiny purple berries. A two-winged red maple seed floats in a backwater, looking from a distance like a drowning red butterfly. The forest hosts a celebration of seed and berry.

The crows are watching me. When their grating cry rings out again, I know I'm still the object of their curiosity and conversation and I start to feel guilty for trespassing in a private world full of wild secrets, creature language and hidden territory. But at the same time I feel the visceral excitement of being witnessed and studied in an alien world where the tangible feeling of being scrutinized perks my awareness. This heightened alertness comes from attention paid to me by creatures, trees and plants, even if I don't know who or what is watching. I am seen. When I keenly observe nature, nature returns the favor.

Other birds awaiting my departure have either fallen silent or left the area and the riverbank is quiet except for bumblebees, who won't stop their busy work for anyone. Plus the band tailed pigeon who assures me everything is fine and I am more than welcome.

To reach the Hood Canal I push aside seven-foot high reeds, press down thorny brambles and wild rose branches, stopping frequently to marvel at the ecstatic busyness of thousands of honeybees crawling over blackberry blossoms. The path from our Beard's Cove bee yard to the hook end of the Hood Canal is completely overgrown, but with pushing and stomping persistence, I succeed in tunneling a narrow alleyway just wide enough for me to reach the tidelands.

At the shoreline I'm hit by the sour, briny smell of rotten sea vegetation, muck and flotsam in messy entanglement with acres of sea-arrow grass, tules and sedges that tuft the marshy end of the canal. Between reeds, ebb tide rivulets crawl snakelike in shy skins of receding water that etch the wide expanse of low tide mud flats. A downy duck feather, caught on top of a reed, flutters in the breeze like a surrender flag above an army of bayonet rushes. Rotted driftwood disintegrates underfoot. A scrawny spruce, dressed with rows of rust colored cones and new green growth, stands gnarled and proud like a decorated war veteran in full regalia. I lie back against the old spruce trunk, relax and bask in the salt marsh sunshine.

Making my way back to the bee yard, with far less struggle after reclaiming the path, I pause again to marvel at crowds of bees gorging on blackberry nectar, then wander to nearby wild black raspberry bushes where I gorge on handfuls of ripe berries. What is it about berry picking that is so satisfying? Successful wild berry foraging always evokes feelings of well-being and wealth.

By the time I arrive back at the yard, grass seeds cling to my sweaty neck and stick to my arms, especially inside the elbows. Blood trickles from scratched legs and berry juice stains my fingers. I look more like a kid returning from wild woodland adventures than a mature adult on an afternoon stroll.

And, like any kid on a summer's day, I'm ready to plunge into cold clear water. A small lake and campground hide in the State Forest close to our property. If we're lucky, we visit on a day with no drunken parties, loud voices and dust spewing RVs. This year, with the campsite loop road closed, visitors must carry their gear in from the parking lot, and perhaps the campground will be quieter. Today we're lucky. Only one subdued young family lounges by the water.

Reflections ripple waffles of light that weave black, silver and gold across the lake. I dive in and shatter the pattern. Close to shore, sun-heated surface currents warm the upper half of my body; further out, cool under-currents swirl around my legs like streamers of sinuous weed. The pebbled bottom is clearly visible. Tiny darting fishes hover, then nibble at my toes. I roll and tumble and play, splash armfuls of spray and wallow in sensual layers of warm and cool water, a large aquatic animal immersed in lapping waves.

I float. I float. And I float, languidly, lazily letting go into the buoyant bliss of drifting water. I relax on my back, ears underwater in the silence, fingers laced behind my head for a pillow, toes and nipples above the surface. I float like a piece of driftwood, a lotus leaf, a duck, a flower petal, a half-submerged sea mammal with flippers in the air. I listen to the sound of my breath and melt into primordial water-womb comfort. I lounge and drift contented through the warm late afternoon in easy surrender to the clean, gentle lake water. This is truly paradise. For a short while, no thoughts interrupt about the darker side of our community.

Reluctantly at nightfall we drive away from the lake. A pickup passes us headed for the campground, tires spinning hard on the bumpy dirt road, kicking up clouds of dust. Five wild-looking teenagers hang from the truck bed, rap music pumps from the cab. I doubt they are visiting the lake for the kind of relaxation I prefer. Our timing is good.

☼

A warm night. The full moon rises around 10:30pm as we drive to Wild Lily Lake. Salal, ferns and grasses disguise the track to where we park. Our privacy is assured.

In warm darkness we stumble and slide down a deer trail to the water's edge. Behind us, a southern hill hides the low moon, but soft light glows among treetops that line the opposite northern shore. We spread a blanket and lean back against a bank to watch the rising moon show, awaiting the main attraction, the full moon reflected on a lotus lake.

The opening act draws out long and entertaining. For two hours, dozens of amorous bullfrogs compete to attract mates

157

with rhythmic improvisations that punctuate the silence every two or three seconds. Deep booms reverberate from far off lily pads, certain to impress female frogs with maturity and self-assurance, while other high and perky mating calls, definitely from awkward teenage studs, croak nearby.

A minimalist score of little sounds plays against a background of alternating bullfrog operetta and penetrating quiet: scratching, rustling, night bird cries, peeps, squeaks, pops, splashes and the incessant high pitched whine of circling mosquitoes.

But the shy full moon continues to hide behind skirts of the southern hillside, only lighting the far side of the lake. Above, stars shimmer in the hazy moonlight. Bats swoop across the water's surface, gorging on low-flying insects. A nighthawk breaks out in a shrill cry.

For hours we wait for the moon to emerge bravely above the hill and trees behind us. But she won't leave her hiding place. There will be no full moon reflection tonight on the black night lotus lake, for her milky path travels too low across the southern sky. Japanese poets often revered the magic and soulful mystery of moonlight and her fleeting shadows more than the Moon herself. Contented with the moonlit reverie of shadow play and night sound, we slip easily under the magic spell of Wild Lily Lake and doze off in the quiet, lulled by hypnotic whisperings until a rush of treetop wind awakens us, reminding us that it is time to leave this lake of moon shadows.

After lashing our new two-person rubber dinghy to the top of my Subaru, we head for the nearest small lake. Both lake and campground are deserted even though only 6pm, the weather warm, and still two more hours of daylight.

The dinghy glides out over smooth water, the lake silent except for the drip of oars. A kingfisher, then a nighthawk, sweeps through the early evening sky, then, far off, a pileated woodpecker fires a muffled ratchet. Every so often a fish breaks the surface, rippling small expanded wake. Reeds and lily pads meander arm in arm along the shoreline. Being in a boat, and not in the water, gives a whole different perspective than when I swim or float this beautiful lake.

The boat carries us into a dreamtime that I wish could last forever. Only this lake exists. Clear water, dripping oars, setting sun and a drowsy peace. Time slows as we row, then drift, row, then drift around the perimeter. Shadows lengthen. The sun eases behind dark trees. We forget everything outside the present moment. Where else in the world, at this elevation and so accessible by vehicle, would we find such a friendly lake with no piranha, no poisonous snakes, not many bugs and only the occasional thought reminding me of less than pleasant neighbors?

PART THREE

FALL

CHAPTER 25

GARDEN HARVEST

WITH EVERY summer long-light moment filled with beekeeping or markets—except for essential time-outs at neighborhood lakes—we seldom manage to find the time needed to slow down to prepare and enjoy the garden harvest. We're busy, too busy, selling at farmers markets and eat hurriedly at market food booths or on the road. Only in winter can we savor slow home-cooked meals. But somehow, in our non-stop schedule, I find time to freeze, dry, store or share most of the bountiful harvest from our garden, wild forage and markets. Luckily, we have two freezers (one used primarily for storing bee pollen), and a voluminous food dryer.

August, and the garden is a speeded up movie of plant evolution. My woven harvest basket fills fast with giant zucchini (you know, the ones that race for a world record as soon as one's back is turned), yellow squash, garlic, cucumbers, sugar snap peas, shelling peas, first ripe red and yellow tomatoes, broccoli, kale, bunches of basil and several varieties of lettuce. I top the overflowing veggies with a bouquet of yarrow, lavender, bachelor buttons and marigolds.

After freezing flats of raspberries, I invite the four children from the horse ranch to harvest any leftover berries and watch as, red-lipped and juicy-fingered, they sample fruit down the rows and up again, fill plastic buckets for jam and syrup, and sample again. After they're well-stained red and their buckets full, I take protective netting off the bushes and invite birds to enjoy any berries that escaped kid harvest, and those still to ripen. Raspberries hold a special place in my heart. For a while I owned a small berry farm in Oregon where yearly, at harvest time, I hosted a community 'Raspberry Rendezvous' celebration. An afternoon and evening of raspberry picking became a night of dancing to live bands and camping, before a raspberry pancake breakfast.

After scrubbing mesh shelves of the large food dryer in the woodshed, I harvest basil, oregano, sage, thyme, rosemary, tarragon and marjoram, clean the aromatic leaves and scatter them on the shelves. Early mornings here are often too moist and dewy to air-dry herbs.

☼

Now, in early September, I harvest a volunteer potato crop squatting in a valley between two raised beds. The potatoes range from the size of a thumb nail to a large fist. I did not plant these potatoes. I have never had luck growing potatoes. This surprise crop, probably sprouted from a determined scrap carried from the compost pile, arrives to prove me otherwise, despite an ambitious crowd of other weedy squatters. Again, I marvel at the unpredictable generosity of nature. Other crops haven't fared as well. Beets are meager, I suspect because their bed is too close to a shady plum tree, and amaranth hasn't reached the anticipated height of five-to-six-foot.

The garden sizzles with the fall rhythm of crickets; an audience of twittering birds perch on beanpoles; a sudden chorus of barks, yelps and howls from a coyote pack by the river reminds me of life outside the garden. Zap joins in. After a minute the coyote chorus ends as abruptly as it began and garden sounds return to sizzle and twitter.

I sweep my hand along old kale stems and fill a paper bag with bursting seedpods. The brittle pods snap and pop and shower black seeds into the bottom of the sack. Within five minutes I have half-a-pint of kale seed to plant next spring.

For dinner tonight, the rare occasion of an at-home meal: a starter salad of tomatoes, cucumber, chives and parsley. For the main course: steamed green beans, broccoli, parsnip, chard and green and yellow zucchini, served with a basil and garlic sauce. For a table centerpiece, a bouquet of orange amaranth, marjoram, rue, red and white yarrow, echinacea and sage.

☼

Cirrus clouds streak the basic blue sky. I lie on my back, slightly uncomfortable, on the warm lawn. Lawn grass, no longer soft and green, has dried to prickly straw. I turn my attention to September sounds.

Crickets lay down a hypnotic rhythm while, nearby, a single bumblebee hums from dandelion to dandelion. An erratic yellow jacket arrives to investigate the prone figure on the lawn, brushes cool wings against my arm, makes quick forays over my clothes and moves on. Two crows hold a truncated conversation, one squawk followed by a brief three-squawk response; a fly drones past; squirrels, intent on expanding winter stockpiles, squeak and chatter in firs; a lone cricket clicks close-by. A savage jet rips the sky. After echoes of the thunderous intrusion fade, my world returns to the sound of falling leaves. Regardless of whatever crimes our neighbors might be committing, they do keep quiet.

I walk around the clearing, noting how tree shadows have lengthened across the lawn. Each year, as trees grow taller, the clearing becomes more shaded. The untidy thistle patch bends low, half green, and half brown; wads of fluffy down lie sodden and matted on the ground while last silken tufts cling to damaged stems. Summer snakes have vanished from the snake path to snuggle and entwine in their underground nest, while above ground, bees scrutinize any half-alive blossom for a last chance at nectar, knowing that winter approaches and harvest time is short.

Only one out of the nine orchard apple trees bears fruit from still leafy branches. Some years we pick bushels of apples, but not this year. Perhaps the trees were over-pruned, pruned at the wrong time for a crop this season, or maybe last year's rain fell in the wrong season. Two pear trees lament a pitiful harvest of wormy rotten fruit. But the Italian plum trees in the garden, that never fail us, drop fat plums with every gust of wind. I fill my basket with purple windfall before insects discover, disfigure and devour the fallen fruit. Plum branches shade an ever-larger portion of the garden each year courtesy of the gift of free sprinkler spray. Rivulets run from leaves creating paddy fields at the drip line, much appreciated by young self-seeded trees. Perhaps the pear and apple trees could use a bonus of free sprinkler spray too.

I stand back and evaluate grapevines climbing relentlessly over one of the larger plum trees like ivy intent on obliterating an old wall. Some grapevines creep to another enclosure where choking tendrils threaten a Japanese maple, while other vines wander beyond the garden fence, only to be subjected to radical pruning by deer that love the tannin in the tender foliage. Pink sedum flowers in the Japanese garden have also been subjected to radical pruning.

When we return from an evening trip to the store, a deer crosses the driveway and two more stare into our headlights from the lawn. Deer are entitled to sanctuary on our property during hunting season.

In the morning I find just how much sanctuary deer have found in our clearing. Feeling right at home, with no human threatening to chase them away, they jumped the high garden fence and feasted almost entirely through the grapes, kale, ripe tomatoes and plums. At least they haven't figured out how to dig for juicing carrots. I can't really blame the deer for recognizing the quality food source of a good garden, but next year, I'll raise the fence considerably higher. Deer munching and recent frost have taken a toll and the garden spirals downhill fast.

I protect the remainder of the tomato crop by laying tomato trellises on the ground, knowing that the wire will spook the deer (it has worked before). The garden has provided more than we can use this year so I don't mind if animals share the last of our bounty. And pruning the grapevine will be easy. But I do rescue and transplant surviving kale plants and throw a net over them until I learn another method of deer prevention.

At the base of an echinacea plant I find a sizeable hole, an entry to an underground home. A mole? A rat? Rabbit? Mountain beaver? To me it looks like an entrance to a tunnel for Shamanic journeying to consult animal guides. If I took a journey down the hole I might ask a guide about effective deer communication or deterrents. And we still need answers to the ominous situation that hovers over the community.

In the evening a woman calls Roy asking advice about a hornet's nest. During their conversation he mentions the deer invasion. She suggests wicks saturated in ammonia, placed in bud vases. Or a stinking blend of rotten eggs. How quickly answers come! Now if only a solution to the neighborhood predicament would arrive as fast.

☼

Fluttering from every corner of the garden in pink misty morning light, a flock of sprightly juncos announce seed pecking time.

Deer ignored the kale transplanted yesterday, and my tomato protection was successful. Only the grapevines look slimmer and the deer are welcome to the vines before they swallow the plum trees. The deer seem to know and honor the boundaries I set. Yes to vines, no to kale and tomatoes. Non-verbal communication is received more readily than I expect. Perhaps non-verbal boundaries I've set with the neighbors have protected our property, though I'll have to work harder on protection from invasive thoughts.

I shake amaranth seed heads over a bag, first results of my attempt to grow a cereal. I don't expect a large harvest for the first year of a new crop, but learn about the plant from

167

observing its likes and dislikes. From this year's amaranth observations I learn that the soil is adequate, but the plants would appreciate more space, more sunshine, less weeds, and less water. Not exactly scientific, but simple and workable.

Handfuls of cherry tomatoes drop from plants as I pluck the ripest ones. Fruit turns shiny red even though the vines are black and wilted. I harvest skinny parsnips and fat juice carrots and pull dried bean pods off dying bean vines.

Cricket song permeates the woods. As I raise the garage door a cricket creeps from his hiding place underneath, surprised in his search for a winterized home. A frog chirps in the distance. Squirrels peep up and down trees. With each wind gust, crackling alder leaves flutter down in slow motion.

I relax on the lawn and husk amaranth heads, straining the seeds through a sieve. Almost as much chaff as seed falls through the mesh, but I succeed in blowing away the chaff without losing the tiny seeds. Even with the negligible amount I winnow for a couple of breakfasts, I proudly call my first cereal growing experiment a success. Next, I brush dirt off a bagful of chanterelles with a stiff paintbrush, break up the mushrooms and fill two trays in the dehydrator.

After cleaning out the workshop flowerbed and wheeling a pungent barrowful of horse manure from across the road, I add another barrow of fresh soil from under the compost pile and plant a hundred 'exotic mixed' tulips for a splash of color. Behind the tulips I sow orange tiger lily seeds collected in the mountains.

Attacking weeds around the raspberry bushes, I rip out grass and thistles by the handful and cut away dead raspberry stalks that fruited this year. New stalks forecast next year's robust raspberry crop.

Following a seasonal rhythm, I choose small tokens to decorate our dining room table. Today it's anise hyssop, dried teasel, sage, dill and echinacea seed heads.

I roll up garden hoses and pull out stakes to clear the path for rototiller blades, then weed and mulch around echinacea, yarrow, lavender, penstemon and valerian.

With winter approaching, jars of honey stored on pallets in the garage have begun to crystallize. During the coldest months we store bottled honey in the heated extractor room or in the warmth of our home. This evening I pile wood into the living room wood stove, light the first fire of the year and place honey jars on tiles near the heat to slowly warm the crystallized honey back to flowing gold.

Garden chores complete for another year, I stand between vegetable beds and look back on so many hours of pleasurable garden work (yes, even the weeding), and an abundant harvest, with a heart overflowing with gratitude.

CHAPTER 26

Olympic Explorations

WHILE DRIVING along the south shore of the Hood Canal to pull honey from hives above Hoodsport, we pass the neighbors' white Mustang parked by a row of mailboxes. Lights flash on a Sheriff's vehicle parked behind the Mustang. Several mailbox doors hang open. Another car, one we have also seen on the neighbors' property, waits in tree shadows on the other side of the road. We keep driving, guessing whether or not the neighbors are about to be arrested for diving into mailboxes not their own. We find it hard to understand why nothing has yet been done to investigate their blatant criminal activity. Maybe this will end their thieving ways.

Etching a silhouette at the low tide water's edge of the Hood Canal, a motionless heron knows that Chinook are running and his patience will be rewarded. Indian fishing nets hang from floats across the river upstream from the Skoke Bridge.

Downstream, below the bridge, standing chest-high in river water in a row four to five feet apart, eighteen fishermen in waders cast their lines. A bite! A salmon leaps, twists, flashes and curves through the air to escape the swallowed barb. The lucky fisherman yells upstream to the others to pull in their lines. The big salmon weaves and struggles, the rod bends and strains; the battle is on, a race of exertion and exhaustion. We think we know who will win but won't stay to watch the results. We have our own work ahead.

Young summer-grown alder scrape the underside of the pickup as we climb the rocky road into the mountains. New vegetation takes hold fast on little used logging roads.

We reach the first bee yard and sigh with relief to find the hives and fence undisturbed. No bears, no vandals.

The temperature is cool, the air damp with first signs of fall. Clouds puff ragged through mountain peaks. Fog and cloud droplets bead leaves and petals. We expect only one more week of fireweed as pink flowers open higher and higher up maroon stems, leaving behind slender pods ready to shower feather-down fluff. A handful of diligent bees suck wet fireweed for a drop of nectar, some settle for false dandelion, while others fill pollen baskets from pearly everlasting growing thick beside the high logging roads.

Roy harvests pollen from pollen trap drawers under hive boxes that bees must pass through to reach the frames. Most of this week's pollen is dusty purple/gray from fireweed, speckled with gold and orange pellets from the pearly everlasting. We sample pinches of the fresh, sweet, soft pollen delicacy that crumbles and melts on the tongue. Pollen—"food of the Gods', 'ambrosia', 'manna'—rich in protein and amino acids, contains enough nutritional value to sustain life.

I wander from the bee yard sampling berries from bushes on either side of the road: red huckleberries, mountain blueberries, both too tart; thimbleberries, blackberries and blackcap raspberries, just right. Other red and black berries tempt seductively, but with only guesswork as to whether or not they're poisonous, I resist their flirtation.

Finding a dry spot on a lichen-covered rock to gaze across the steep valleys, I instantly land in a Chinese watercolor where dragon clouds whisper among weathered firs sprung from craggy cliffs. The only thing missing is a pair of cranes.

On our way back from the quick trip to the mountains, a group of flickers swoop and flap downhill above the truck. Birds prepare for fall and winter travel. At Hwy 101 in Hoodsport the sky clears and the sinking sun throws a pearly pink/turquoise sheen over the surface of the Canal. The tide is high. Salmon fishermen on the Skoke have all left, maybe with a Chinook or two.

When we arrive home, both the neighbors and their vehicles are back on their property. No arrests. Either that or they were immediately freed on bail.

Labor day. We drive again to the Olympics in our little red Toyota to harvest pollen and to search for possible future bee yard sites. Pollen collection is a twice-weekly trip at this time of year to satisfy eager customers who line up for fireweed honey and fresh pollen at five farmers markets a week. Last week our pollen supply sold out within the first hour of each market. Fresh pollen isn't widely available and most people have only tasted freeze-dried pollen that pales in comparison to the flavor and nutrition of pollen straight from a hive.

Storm winds whip whitecaps along the Canal. Disappointed sailors and fishermen have given up battling waves. Oversize vehicles towing large boats crawl homeward. A pickup passes us pulling a trailer loaded with a giant-wheeled off-road jeep. In 1984 Edward Abbey wrote: "One punk slob on a dirt bike makes more noise takes up more space inflicts more damage than a hundred horsemen or a thousand walkers" (Confessions of a Barbarian, Journal XVIII). He'd turn in his grave if he saw this monster.

We drive with caution up the old logging road to our yard, concerned that at any moment a speeding vehicle might swoop down around a bend, but we need not worry, we don't meet any traffic. Discouraged campers and hikers have all fled for the comfort of home. Ragged clouds close in around mountain peaks above the bee yard.

We empty the pollen traps. This time the pollen is all gold and orange pellets from pearly everlasting. Pollen season is almost over, and by the end of the week we'll remove all the traps. With cool weather since the last collection, the quantity of pollen has dropped sharply and any pollen crumbs salvageable from fading flowers will be left as valuable winter food for the bees.

Three years ago, as we drove home one evening after a market we spotted smoke plumes billowing from ridges and valleys along the western horizon and were immediately worried for the safety of our hives in the mountains. The forest wildfire burned for a week in the Brothers Wilderness of the Olympics. Luckily the burn was several miles north of our yards and the bees unharmed, although probably bothered by the smoke. After the fire, Roy contacted the Forest Service to secure a lease on land close to the burn area when fireweed re-seeds.

Today we will explore back roads in the high country to see if fireweed has seeded yet on the burned acreage and how close we can drive to the fire site. We're searching for a location blanketed in summer with pink blossom, ready to welcome millions of bees. A location easily accessible with the big flatbed truck.

We cross the Hamma Hamma River. At the end of a dry summer the Hamma Hamma is a shallow stream broken by lichen-dappled rocks. Luminous turquoise water bubbles around the rocks. Where flow to the central channel has dried up, brackish pools evaporate in smooth basins. Pristine moss, fern and reddening vine maple overhang the banks. The rocks, river and vegetation could easily be a Japanese Zen garden.

A sign reads 'Steep Narrow Winding' at the bottom of an old logging road where we hope to access the burn area. We start up the steep incline. And yes, the sign is accurate. But someone forgot to add the words 'Bumpy, Full of Holes and Scarier than Hell when you Look Over the Side'.

Timber harvested from these steep Olympic forests during early decades of logging created millionaires and supplied the whole world with logs. I am in awe of pioneering loggers who risked their lives to harvest trees from the precipitous hillsides. And many did die or lose a limb. I doubt that the millionaires were among those who worked the slopes.

At a fork in the road we pause for a snack of ripe thimbleberries. Two fat quail waddle in front of the truck then hop onto a nearby branch. Along the top of a ridge to our left, burned tree spires jut like black needles along the mountain skyline. We choose the left fork.

Rocks and boulders block half the road to discourage travelers but Roy decides the road isn't closed and inches the truck around the obstacle. This is not a place for height phobia. Steep ravines plummet from the narrow track. Nervous about what lies ahead, I urge caution, especially after we lurch over three half-cleared rockslides and I peer at the don't-forget-to-breathe view over the road's edge. If the truck cannot turn around, we will have to back down. That would not be a good idea.

A touch of hysteria prompts me to bail out. Roy can pick me up on his way back.

After the sound of the pickup disappears around a bend, I am left in a vast silence. Except for Roy, there is not another soul for miles and miles. Probably less than half-a-dozen people venture up here each year.

Massive walls on the mountain side of the road overwhelm me, and I hardly dare look to the other side. Ant-like, humbled, and very alone, I hug cliff-side boulders and avoid peering over the sheer drop as I gingerly pick through fallen rocks and boulders. I felt safer in the pickup, not as immediately aware of the dangers as I am now. In today's high winds I pray that precarious stumps and rocks don't fall as I walk underneath. But I tell myself that rain, and not wind, would be more likely to loosen sandy earth and cause a rock or landslide.

Biting mountain wind sweeps through gnarled firs that cling to the bare rock. The tenacity of the trees reassures me. In the distance a male grouse boasts his distinctive and somewhat comforting thwoom, thwoom, thwoom. I relax and finally remember to breathe deeply.

Bushes of blackcap raspberries, my all-time favorite wild berry, sprawl beside the road. Fears dissipate as soon as purple blotches stain my fingers and pants. A clump of wild tiger lilies have finished blooming and I shake seeds from their brittle pods to take home, wondering if they will grow at a lower altitude. Maidenhair ferns spray and tumble from the hillside, the fern aptly named for dangling black straggly roots that look like dreadlocks. Before long, embraced by nature, I enjoy my aloneness on the wilderness mountainside.

But I am relieved when I hear the approaching rumble of the pickup returning down the mountain. Roy barely managed to turn around by an impassable landslide of uprooted trees and rocks. I'm glad he had to turn back. The idea of driving the big boom truck up here loaded with bees next year borders on insanity. Maybe another road might offer easier access to the burn area. But we will wait till spring to find out.

☼

Three days later and we again climb the road to bee yards above Lake Cushman. Playful cloud billows and vaporous fingers curl through steep-sloped fir forests. By the time we reach the first yard giant raindrops splash the dusty road. A single thunderous drum-roll slaps, then reverberates around the ragged peaks. We won't attempt to pull honey in this weather. We would have to brush bees from individual frames and the bees would be unnecessarily stressed. We drive on to the next yard only to check on the bees, not to take any honey. The bees are happy, humming along inside the hives, housecleaning, rearranging stores, managing the environment for the coming winter months.

Then we must decide whether to head north along the Canal to the Quilcene bee yard. Can we beat the storm? Dramatic weather is moving north, but if the storm track stays in high mountains to the west, Quilcene should be in sunshine. We decide to give it a try.

Taking the back road to the Hamma Hamma we drop through mystical valleys where wreaths of wispy cloud drift and vanish through fir and hemlock. We feel as if we are the only people in the eastern slopes of the Olympics, wrapped in dissolving cotton-candy fluff that softens every contour of the rugged terrain. At the edge of the approaching storm, light raindrops shimmer through ravines and green shadowed hillsides.

On the valley floor by the Hood Canal, we must choose whether to continue north or return home. An untidy mix of cloud and sunshine splatters the sky, and to the north, black clouds slide eastward from high peaks to the foothills. We vote for home. To continue to Quilcene would be a waste of time. As soon as we choose home the sky paints a pastel rainbow over the mouth of the Hamma Hamma.

The three boys who live on the horse ranch across the road are missing. The children, age eight, nine and ten, disappear during the afternoon, after they boldly told their grandma they're going fishing in the creek with handmade wooden spears. She has instructed them to stay in the yard, but twenty minutes later, when grandma calls for them, they're gone. Everyone in the neighborhood (except our immediate neighbors), joins the search. For an hour and a half the grandma shouts and whistles within a mile radius, but no boys.

Joining the search, we hike back through another neighbor's property across low-lying brush toward a county road, looking for the boys. Making a loop around, we cross two creeks, then check our stretch of river. Still no sign of the boys.

Night falls. Sharon keeps calling for the missing boys till her voice is hoarse. She is terrified that men from the neighboring meth labs may have kidnapped them to spite her. Even though none of us say anything aloud, we all share similar fears. Eventually the police arrive with truckloads of volunteers, equipped with maps and headlamps, ready for a full-scale search and rescue operation.

At six fifteen, the boys are picked up, walking along a dirt road in the dark more than five miles from home. After leaving their yard, they crossed the fishing creek on a fallen trunk. The trunk dislodged, and the creek was too wide to jump back across the fast deep water. Creek sides were too steep to walk to a bridge upstream, which would have easily led them home. So they hiked downstream, scrambled up the bank, found a dirt road, took off in the wrong direction and quickly became lost. After an hour they reached a closed campground where they found a map on a notice board and were able to figure out how to reach another campground. A group of dirt bike riders at the second campground directed them to the county road where a passing driver picked them up.

Sharon is close to hysterical, and everyone else upset, but the boys are fine, only cold and wet, and the youngest a little scared. They knew that they were OK in the woods. When asked what they learned from their experience, one of the boys replies, "I'd take a coat next time!"

CHAPTER 27

Mushroom Time

SPIDER WEBS float from every branch, twig, railing, window ledge, stalk and leaf. Backlit by sunlight, a fat brown orb weaver spins a web outside the dining room window. I watch her every move. Gossamer thread flows in a stream from her belly as she hooks the thread from spoke to spoke with her two hind legs, thirty-seven spokes in all. Working with amazing speed and skill she weaves her web round and round from the perimeter to the center till she has spun forty-eight rounds in her spiral dance. With the snare complete, she rests in the middle of her masterpiece, dreaming of fresh fly dinner. The whole web hangs two-foot long by eighteen inches wide.

A splattering of rain fell three days ago, sprouting first mushrooms of the season. I head to Tall Trees Trail to harvest chanterelles. Entering the woods, I slow down and tune myself to the healing forest silence before beginning my search. I know where to look first. Old fir and cedar overshadow moss carpets where minimal sunshine filters to the forest floor of matted roots, fallen twigs and fir needles. That is where chanterelles will show themselves.

Almost immediately I spot two small yellowish fluted trumpets. Then large white clusters beckon. Each time I glance in another direction chanterelles appear at the edge of my field of vision. I find that the indirect attention of peripheral sight works best for mushroom hunting, and soon, the plastic bag tied to my belt loop hangs heavy with chanterelles. Wandering a hundred yards further into the shaded depths of the forest where I've found them before, I stop frequently to investigate all small yellow and orange-brown objects, often only dead Oregon grape leaves, and even though another mushroom hunter has left a trail of cut chanterelle stems, my bag soon bounces full against my hip.

I hike further down the trail avoiding fresh black/purple mounds of coyote droppings, full of seed from a berry-packed diet. Not bothered by my presence, a downy woodpecker plays hide and seek, pecks up a fir trunk, then down, then disappears below a cover of bracken. He hops up again tapping at the bark with his sharp beak.

When I leave the forest, three pickups are parked by the entrance to Tall Trees Trail. Others also know the right time and place to harvest chanterelles. Lucky I arrived first.

☼

A month has passed since I last visited Wild Lily Lake and now, in fall, the lake speaks a language of desolate beauty. Water level has lowered two feet, baring gnarled snags blackened by months of immersion. Ravaged limbs protrude at weird angles, muddy from ooze and low water slime. Sparse dirty plants shoot from new mud islands for a brief show of life before rain falls and lake water rises to drown their brave effort, and across most of the surface, pondweed and lilies are now tangles of reddish root, tubers and swaying stems. Insect-ridden golden lily flowers disintegrate, shadows of former royal selves. The previously peaceful vista is still peaceful but has shape shifted to a haunted swamp of decaying vegetation as life energy sinks to roots beneath the dark surface.

As I approach the lakeshore the peace shatters abruptly. I am startled by, and startle, hundreds of frogs, newts and other little aquatic creatures. They leap from lookout platforms, basking pads and hunting docks and plunge into the murky water. Squeak plop! Multiplied a hundredfold. I am reminded of

Basho's Zen haiku about the sound of a frog plopping into an ancient pond, but this scene is anything but Zen. Frantic peeps, croaks and splashes echo across the pond. Water ripples and dimples after the fleeing frogs as their powerful legs thrash and dash across the surface till they dive under rotting leaves, mud, reeds and weeds. Anywhere to hide from this enormous intruder. Plant energy might be dwindling, but frogs, insects and dragonflies are in their prime.

Turquoise and red dragonflies dart and swoop over the pond like iridescent helicopters, snatching morsels from the hovering cloud of fall bug harvest. The air whines with the buzz of insects, yellow jackets and mean-looking bald-faced hornets competing for their next life-sustaining meal. A languid heron flaps to the far side of the water.

Lily leaves alchemize a patina of metallic yellow, red and bright green. Underneath, feathery milfoil and jelly green weed shuffle in the floating ooze. Scummy muck edges up the shore.

Interpreting tales of multi-layered tracks that criss-cross a three-foot wide mud moat, I meander around the living/dying lake circumference. Coyote pads interrupt smaller raccoon prints. Deer and heron prints give other clues. And now my boots add another storyline. Occasionally my heels crunch with a sound I am too familiar with, the crackle of crumpled aluminum. Where water has receded, bullet-punctured beer cans and plastic bottles tell yet another story.

My daughter-in-law Rose and her aunt, both Malaysian from Sabah on the island of Borneo, visit for the day. After a quick garden tour we head to Tall Trees Trail for an introduction to mushroom hunting. We don't have to look far. As soon as we leave the trail, clumps of large white chanterelles show themselves. The visitors hunt with the confident knowing of experts. Or is it just beginner's luck and we've picked a perfect day for mushroom hunting? Bags fill fast. Mushrooms push up everywhere, from smallest porcelain fairy caps to a stand of huge brown russulas that threaten to dwarf the petite aunt, who, with silken black hair flowing to her knees and elegant long fingers, looks completely at home in the enchanted elfin scene where she crouches beside the giant mushrooms.

Cool drizzle awakens mushroom heaven in the forest. As deciduous leaves crumble and disintegrate, masses of fungi and lichen spring to life in the shadowy evergreen underworld. Every few inches a fleshy umbrella shades the greening moss, although it is already shady enough. Button type mushrooms weigh down tall bent stalks. Coral mushrooms and dozens of wine-red russula erupt in the dimly lit green moss ocean. Small animal tooth-prints graze russula skins laying bare the white inner flesh. Even as we walk through the woods, mushrooms leap up around us and I can almost hear them growing: slimy pinkish, glossy white, all shades of brown, copper, tan, some rough and round, some like Japanese parasols, and one petite lavender cap. Mushrooms stage a spectacular Vaudeville show above the velvety moss. At the forest edge, a quartet of amanitas, one large warty orange umbrella and three red speckled puffballs, closely guard our mailboxes with their poisonous bright shine. Three other amanita stems have been cut and I wonder if neighbors have been experimenting with a psychotropic brew.

As we hike the ferny river trail beyond the forest, both women exclaim how they're reminded of tropical Mount Kinabalu slopes in northern Borneo where many of the same ferns grow, especially sword ferns. But there is a difference. Walks in their homeland forests include deadly and dangerous snakes and insects. Here, they find it hard to believe that snakes and caterpillars are harmless in the friendly temperate northwest. I only briefly mention my fears about our own dangerous northwest forest inhabitants, our neighbors.

☼

The next day Roy, Ian and I go to harvest mushrooms near 'the pond' summer bee yard. Roy and Ian disappear into closely-knit forest beside a stream to search for chanterelles and then target practice while I take off in the opposite direction and dive through willow bushes to explore a string of beaver ponds.

Undergrowth shambles thick and dusty. Before long, faced by an impenetrable wall of huckleberry bushes and unable to find an animal trail to scramble through, I'm forced to give up my exploration, at first annoyed by my thwarted plan. But my eyes soon widen at the sight of thousands of ripe huckleberries and I immediately switch to an alternative plan as visions of steaming huckleberry pancakes with melting honey flash through my mind. I draw my fingers along huckleberry stems hung with the small ripe berries, grabbing fistfuls of the shiny dark fruit until my hands and mouth are berry-juice-purple and my bag half full with a huckleberry harvest.

A pickup swerves past on the dirt road close to my brushy cover. The truck throws up a cloud of dust, then stops a hundred yards away. A door slams. I go on picking. Perhaps it's another mushroom hunter or berry picker.

Distant shots ring out as Roy and Ian target practice in the forest. Then Kapow! A shot explodes closer, much closer, right by the pond. I immediately stop berry picking, scramble up the slope to the road and take cover behind our pickup. I am in no mood to be mistaken for a deer. More shots blast nearby. The place is a war zone, not a peaceful forest for picking berries and mushrooms.

On hearing the shots, Roy and Ian rush back through the trees. With deer hunting season approaching, target practice is a popular pastime. Stray bullets are an expected hazard.

Ian holds up two shopping bags loaded with chanterelles and I realize that I would rather have mushrooms and berries than a dead deer, any day.

CHAPTER 28

Neighborhood Enigma

TWO SQUEALING cats, like cartoon characters with electrified hair, leap from the end of the neighbors' driveway and race past me down the road as I walk by their property. I jump, tense and nervous, and the thought crosses my mind that the cats were released to scare me.

But once past the property I leave the road, push through brush to Tall Trees Trail to gather chanterelles, and relax in the soulful depths of green.

But I am not alone. A paunchy middle-aged man greets me at the entrance to the trail and announces that his partner, a woman in a blue coat, is missing in the forest. They have been picking mushrooms since eight this morning. Now it is two o'clock and he expected her back at his pickup by noon. The man claims that he is in 'state land management' and that he and his partner are in the process of 'taking over this area'. They are brush pickers and mushroom hunters. I tell him I'll keep an eye open for his missing partner. He dives off into the forest in the opposite direction from where I plan to harvest my evening meal.

My mood deteriorates as I imagine gruesome scenarios with the missing mushroom picker as victim. Did our neighbors kidnap her? Did she surprise them in a drug deal? Did she have a heart attack? Will I trip over a leg? Will I find a torn blue coat? But the woman is probably just lost without a watch, unaware of time in these timeless woods. I reign in my increasingly overactive, jittery and paranoid imagination.

I search for chanterelles beneath overgrown stumps and nurse logs where I usually fill a bag right away, but today not a single little yellow trumpet shows itself. Perhaps the blue-coated woman has scoured the woods and vanished with all of them, leaving none for nearby residents who would enjoy a handful for dinner. Or perhaps the end of the season is near.

Ten minutes later, as I hunt in thick undergrowth near the path, the 'lost' woman wanders up the trail with two five-gallon buckets brimful of chanterelles. I approach and relay the message that her friend is looking for her. She snaps back "I know the area well. I ain't lost!" She yanks a whistle out from under her shirt and blasts three times. The piercing sound splits the forest silence like a sharp axe, startling me, and probably every living creature within half a mile, the trees too. The woman might know the area well, but she has a problem with time. And with sensitivity to woodland life.

I leave the forest empty handed, feeling like a fly fisherman whose secret fishing hole has been overrun by noisy tourists.

Sharon from the horse ranch is walking her grandchildren home from the bus stop.

"What was that about?" she asks.

"Just another lost soul in the woods."

Sharon is hunched over, looks tired and stressed out.

"How are you Sharon?"

"I'll be doing a whole lot better once something's done about the neighbors."

"Yeah, but what can we do? If the cops won't do anything, what kind of a plan can we come up with that's reasonable? How're we going to deal with this? We all know something's terribly wrong." I shrug and sigh. I feel helpless. I don't have a solution.

"I'm scared for the kids. People are coming and going at all hours, every night now, loading, unloading, walking around with flashlights. More and more, right out in the open. We can see them from my house." Sharon's house sits directly across the road from the neighbors' driveway. They hate her and her children. They know that she knows what they are up to. She wants them gone. Now.

"The cops don't seem to be investigating, I've made several phone calls," Sharon adds. "We can't just march in and ask them what they're doing."

The countryside used to be thought of as a safe place to raise children, a haven away from shadowy city alleys of gang warfare. Now, northwest woods have become a refuge for criminals and have long been a hiding place for Vietnam vets unable to re-assimilate into society.

The neighbors are not a bunch of misguided kids. They are pros in their 30s and 40s, several of them probably ex-cons, with a sophisticated security system, a pit bull and undoubtedly well armed, but at the same time they operate carelessly in a way that would raise anyone's suspicions. An aura of craziness and danger surrounds them that affects everyone in the community to some degree. We know they're involved in mail theft and we are almost a hundred percent certain they manufacture meth and possibly dump byproducts into the ground. But unless someone enters the property and documents concrete evidence, we have no proof and everything is speculation.

Roy believes that if liquids were being poured out, they would quickly seep through thirty feet of sandy soil into the water table. But he also thinks that the chemicals would 'float' on the surface, not sink or dissolve into the main aquifer since the chemicals used (that he knows of) are lighter than water. So, if our deep well is fifty feet below the surface of the water table, our water should be safe. For now. Whatever way we look at it, it's a terrible scenario.

185

More and more we urgently need to know exactly what is happening next door. I suggest that we make an offer to buy the property from the landowner. Then we would have access to the land to test the soil and water, even if the offer is only a bluff.

Despite several phone calls, the landowner, who lives two hours away, refuses to pay attention to our warnings. Even when we share our fears, suspicions, and what we've witnessed, she shows no interest or desire to investigate her tenants. She has her money. A man and a woman paid up front for a six-month lease when they first moved onto the land. At that time she checked references from phone numbers given to her, and the references appeared acceptable (we later hear they were a scam). We are certain that in the future she will be solely responsible for expensive clean up of a horrific mess and may not be able to rent or sell her land for many years to come.

☼

No one from the sheriff's office shows up to investigate. Phone calls still give no results. Why don't the police act? They tell us they're overloaded with meth cases, so maybe they are understaffed and just too busy. We become increasingly frustrated. As dangerous tensions threaten to escalate into a disaster, a couple of macho vigilante wannabes in our small community say they're ready to take things into their own hands.

Roy strolls up our driveway in the warmth of a late fall night. Half way up the drive he hears a neighbor's voice.

"Did you see that? Did you see that? Get your butt in here," a woman calls urgently from the porch of the mobile home. A man runs from the smaller travel trailer to where she stands.

Roy has triggered motion detectors surrounding their property even though he is well within his own property line, enjoying a quiet evening stroll on his land.

Six months have passed since my encounter with two of the new neighbors in the river valley. Tomorrow their lease is up, but there are no signs of anyone packing and moving out. The community doesn't know where to turn. The landowners do nothing. Police are unresponsive.

Increasingly at night, Roy has nightmares where he sleepwalks, shouts and punches the air. In the long dark evenings he spends more and more time reloading ammunition in the workshop, as his paranoia grows daily.

Finally he has had enough. Extremely upset about being under surveillance on his own property, the incident triggers him to action. Frustrated by lack of response by local law enforcement, he pounds out an email to our congressman, Norm Dicks, describing the increasingly volatile situation. I pray that the urgent letter brings results in time to divert a tragedy.

CHAPTER 29

Bringing Down the Bees

ANOTHER QUICK trip to the Olympic mountains. Approaching the lower bee yard, Roy, his fuse shredded by the neighborhood fiasco and memories of vandalism, mutters "Just pray that no fucking son-of-a-bitch has shot at the hives. And pray more that I don't catch them." Fortunately the first prayer is answered and the second is unnecessary.

Dead and dying drones litter the front of each hive. But this is a natural occurrence. A couple of drones make weak attempts to re-enter the hives, only to be rebuffed by a barrier of worker bees. Before winter, drones are unceremoniously kicked out, a liability no longer worth feeding. They've been freeloading long enough. Drones are only kept around in a hive in case a virgin queen needs a mate to fertilize her eggs and these drones lived longer than those lucky, or unlucky, enough to be the lover of a queen, since mating brings instant death to a drone. I wonder if they know that in advance.

We remove all remaining pollen traps. Each hive now has two deep boxes, ready to band and bring down off the mountain. Most hives are heavy with honey for the cold months ahead, with bees now collecting only minimal nectar and pollen as they suck the last sweet drops of fall. We switch a couple of honey-filled frames to needy hives and head home with the pickup full of unused boxes.

☼

In the driveway, honey-heavy boxes weigh down the flatbed with the last of the year's harvest from the high Olympics. Several hundred bees followed along for the ride, reluctant to leave hard-won honey-packed frames even after the indignities of fume boards and brushing, and now the unloading area outside the workshop is a wild buzz of homeless bees. I tell them to hurry to find shelter in the two kitchen hives but they won't listen.

We wheel the heavy honey boxes through the workshop into the extracting room. For the rest of the day, we extract dark wildflower honey in the hot, sticky and euphorically sweet room where honey drips smear the floor and boxes, and golden liquid flows from stainless steel tanks. Despite picking up frames one by one, paying attention to wandering bees and gently brushing them aside, in a careless moment a bee zaps the palm of my hand. I swear loudly as the sting translates to an immediate flash of anger. Maybe I should pray that I don't get stung. I flick the stinger out, resist swallowing an antihistamine, choosing instead drops of plantain tincture.

☼

Two days ago Roy brought the first load of bees down from the highest mountain yard. Arriving at the yard late, he quickly banded the hives, set entrance closures in place and started loading. But by the time he was half way through, the sky was already dark and he had trouble maneuvering the last three hives onto the truck. He left the three hives hunkered down at the yard, and after driving off the mountain, realized he hadn't pulled closures from those hives.

Our first mountain mission today is to release the captive bees at the high yard. Even with the cool weather when bees don't mind staying inside, they're relieved when we free them into the fall air.

At the next yard we band each hive for moving. Most hives are heavy, brimming with bees and honey. Only a couple are light. A mouse, comfortable in a soft warm nest of fireweed fluff under one hive, will have to find another home. Hornets and yellow jackets hover as we work. Hungry hornets will steal honey and eat bees, and at each hive a small army of guards patrols the landing board ready to defend their property. But the guards leave us alone and only object at one hive as we snap bands around the boxes, and they don't follow us when we move to the next hive. They're far more concerned with the imminent threat of hornets.

A long day lies ahead preparing and moving hives from Quilcene and the Olympics, beginning at the Quilcene bee yard. The slow truck chugs through foothills to Quilcene. Breathing the dry heat of a late fall afternoon through the rolled-down window, I gaze up at copper and gold leaves fluttering against the sear blue sky. Feathered autumn grass quivers in overgrown ditches.

Quiet settles at the bee yard as Roy cuts the noisy boom-truck engine. But the silence doesn't last. After the engine sputters and dies, bee buzz crescendos. The yard vibrates in a frenzy of a million bees scrounging last winter stores, a million bees who want food, and they want it now. The summer hasn't been kind to these bees.

Looking like moonwalkers in our white protective bee suits, we gently tilt hives and slip metal banding under the bottom boxes. But not gently enough. The bees are sensitive and protective of home and honey by this time in the fall. Rightly so. Dozens of sentries rush to attention, hurl themselves against our thin veils to harass us, infuriated by the interruption of their sisters' concentrated hive work.

The assault becomes intolerable. We drop hive tools, leave the yard, disappear into closely grown fir limbs and brush scented needles over our suits to disguise our offensive smell. Loud-buzz guards follow us but soon leave. Quiet returns and we sneak back to band the boxes. Bees pour out, re-group and surge against us, guessing our plan to load them on a heaving, shuddering truck, and they do not want to go. Bees zap Roy multiple times but I am well taped up and protected (thank you, duct tape). Working fast, we finish banding the boxes and leave the angry bees to cool down. We won't move these hives today.

With our planned work for the day only half complete, we leave for higher elevation yards, once again driving the back road up the Hamma Hamma valley where the iridescent river drifts under golden big leaf maples. A soothing interlude after the angry Quilcene bees.

The truck plods up the bumpy unused logging road next to sheer drop-offs to dark ravines. In some places the precipice edge of hairpin bends is badly crumbled. Rocks and dirt from small slides scatter the road. My nervous system jolts when I look down from the high cab to the valley floor. Roy mutters: "Better take a lunch...." and once again I avoid the view. After so many mountain trips I think I should get over my reaction to the stomach turning sight, but I never do.

As we reach the 4,000 ft upper yard by Mount Jefferson, sunset leaks a wash of pale mauve across snow-covered Mount Rainier on the eastern edge of the world. Today, in the fading light, I look all the way across Hood Canal and the Tahuya Peninsula to Tacoma Narrows, the Puget Sound and the Cascades, the first really clear view all year.

After dismantling the bear fence, we uneventfully load the three remaining hives.

By the time we arrive at the next yard, the sky is purple velvet with darkness dropping fast. We pull out flashlights covered with red plastic. Bees can't see infrared, so the light won't bother them. We listen to a pleasurable throbbing hum that rises from deep inside the honey-filled hives. No buzz here, only a mellow hum. These bees are wise to huddle away from the cold night air and they ignore us as we place the wire-mesh closures in hive entrances.

Work is swift and smooth. We load thirty-one hives in the dark, with only five more to go. Soon all thirty-six hives will be strapped to the truck and we'll be off down the mountain.

Wrong!

A three-box hive sways on the mechanical lifter overhead, ready to be lowered onto the truck bed. Roy pushes 'Up' instead of 'Down'. The hive zooms up and slams into the boom. The cable snaps. The hive crashes to the flatbed. Boxes slide apart. Bees crawl, then pour through wide gaps like adrenaline-high fans leaving a stadium. The empty lifter and broken cable swing out, whack my leg and drop to the ground. The dropped hive teeters at the edge of the flatbed.

Roy rushes to force hive boxes back together and pushes the hive away from the edge. Dazed bees swarm over the boxes after the sudden earthquake. We're lucky. Metal banding on the hive holds and the hive doesn't break apart completely or fall off the flatbed. A close call.

Engulfed in a cloud of escaped, and now furious bees, we race to strap down the hives already loaded onto the truck. Inside the hives bees buzz loudly in sympathy with the alarm pheromones of their sisters who just suffered dropped-home-trauma. Roy fields more than twenty stings. I'm fortunate to only be stung twice on my ankle where a sloppy tape job left a crawl space into my hiking boot.

With the cable broken, the boom can't load more hives. We didn't bring the ramp for our hand-truck or our two-person hive lifter, and the hives are too heavy to lift by hand. The remaining hives must be left for another trip.

We drive away from the high wilderness in inky darkness with no moon and no trace of light pollution. Millions of stars sparkle overhead in the vast pitch-black.

Halfway down the mountain we realize that, again, we forgot to remove closures in hives left at the yard. We must return soon to either free the bees or bring them off the mountain. But not tonight.

The beehive-heavy truck lurches down the winding road from the forested mountains, the only vehicle for what seems like hundreds of miles. Headlight beams throw ghostly moving tree shadows. My shin aches from the whack from the lifter. My tired, over-active mind spins out thoughts like seething escaped bees. What if the truck slides over a cliff edge? Should I fasten my seat belt? Or not fasten my seat belt so I can jump to avoid swarming bees in mangled metal? What should I grab first? My flashlight? My water bottle? My bee veil? If I jump, would a tree spear me on the way down? Crucifixion by fir? If I don't jump, would the truck bounce two thousand feet with screams and the deafening crash of metal till sudden silence on the valley floor, then a pause before a rising crescendo of bee buzz? How long would it be before anyone found us? If we survived the fall and millions of angry bees, at least we would have plenty of honey for food. Plus honey to heal our wounds— Romans carried beehives into battle for that very purpose. Thoughts whirl like a tornado. It has been a long day.

☼

The next morning, in daylight, Roy easily fixes the cable on the boom truck and delivers the load of bees to over-winter at the old homestead at Beard's Cove.

A day later: light refreshing rain fell during the night, leaving behind a gentle fog after a long dry spell. We take off early in the small pickup to bring last hives down from the mountains and close the yards for winter.

Along the misty low-tide South Shore of the Canal, wherever a deserted stretch of beach is visible beyond the barriers of hedges, walls, fences and expensive waterfront homes, gray herons stand like statues in alert wading/hunting stance. They are poised to strike, silent, gray against gray beach pebbles, gray water and gray cloud cover. I count sixteen herons. 'Tis the season for fishermen and fisher-birds.

Further south, shining mud flats stretch for miles at the mouth of the Skokomish. Gulls and wading birds waddle and skitter across exposed mud bars, impatient to snag a low-tide breakfast from silt along the snaking sunken river. Below the Skoke Bridge another line of early morning fishermen try their luck for a Chinook. On the Canal west shore, a bald eagle sweeps low above the rocky beach hoping for a salmon supper.

After climbing through a blanket of cloud in the foothills, weak sunshine warms patches of blue. Below us, white oceans roil and froth through valleys. Surging clouds erase the entire Puget Sound. There will be no panoramic view today on our last visit of the year to the Olympics.

At the now tranquil bee yard, so full of drama and distress a couple of nights ago, we unwind the electric fence and pull up fence stakes, then load last of the beehives into the pickup using the two-person hive lifter with no trouble. Work is so much easier in daylight.

Summer and fall visits to this timeless wild land, far away from cities and freeways, are a true gift, and we are immensely grateful for our precious, plentiful pollen and honey harvest. Thank you, dear bees and wildflowers. Our high summer bee yards, where we haven't seen another person all year, are special places of raw windblown rock, trees, wildflowers and limitless views. We are sad to say goodbye to the mountains and Olympic wilderness for another season, but happy to complete our work and close the yards before first snowfall of the year wraps the mountains in white silence.

We leave the Olympic high country for the winter months to bear, elk, mountain goat, lichen, wind and snow. And maybe a handful of adventurous, if perhaps foolish, honeybees who chose to stay.

CHAPTER 30

FI/H

MY SON, Aaron, visits from the city for a vacation. As shadows lengthen in the late afternoon, with our new dinghy securely tied to the top of my station wagon, we drive the winding forested road down to Dewatto Bay.

The beach, where we harvest oysters in winter at low tide, is now entirely submerged at high tide. Wavelets ripple over lower steps of a weathered wood staircase between the road and beach so launching the dinghy is easy. Roy and Aaron row away from shore in a strong wind, the little boat loaded to waterline with two big men, fishing gear and a depth sounder.

While the men muscle their way to the middle of the Canal to play fishermen, I wander off to explore the river mouth. Sun-bronzed grass overhangs banks splashed with over-ripe berries and rosehips. Leaves have lost their summer luster to wilt and wrinkle, to spot and brown with inevitable decay, while insects suck last juices from plants in early stages of dissolution. Life-blood exhausted, vegetation shrinks back to earth.

Close to shore, a rotting half-submerged wooden boat reclines in shallow water with its splintered skeletal hull weighed down by sand, rocks and seaweed. Ebb and flow of tides have long since scrubbed all paint from the boat's curved flanks. The wooden boat, too, shrinks back to earth.

I rest on the beach steps as little waves lap, slap and suck at rocks by my feet. With the wind calmer now, water on the bay undulates in a pattern that dissolves almost as soon as it appears. Silver reflections quiver on the dark surface. Light fades from day to night as the luminous sky morphs a perfect gradient from peach glow on the horizon to light turquoise through to deep Prussian blue overhead. A crescent Moon hovers low, close to Venus, becoming brighter as night slips from twilight to starlight.

Plummeting in sudden dive mode, a nighthawk sounds an abrupt counterpoint to the rhythmic slop and chop of waves. Two herons fly an elegant duet from the mouth of the Dewatto, wings synchronized in black silhouette as they sweep diagonally across my view. Salmon have returned to rivers and streams, to the delight of every fishing bird and man.

The shoreline on the far side of the Canal etches a straight black line. Above the waterline, hills swell dark and mysterious; behind them, a jagged skyline pierces the transparence of a cloudless sky. Below the waterline, light-colored satin waves weave, swell and ripple. Twilight earth floats between sky and water in somber layers of shadow.

Pinpoint lights from far off waterfront homes twinkle on the water as dusk transforms to night. I'm reminded of joyous Greek summer evenings where, as night falls, strings of colored lights reflect on oily island waters and music and dancing celebrate the night.

Excited shouts carry across the water. Fish! When the dinghy reaches shore, well after dark, Aaron and Roy brag about the five fish they caught, throwing four of them back into the Canal. They hold up one good-sized rather ugly rock cod, Aaron's first catch. The first of many yet to come.

☼

Clouds cluster on Olympic ridge tops, and then the whole foggy mass tumbles down to the Canal west of Dewatto. Rain will be here soon. As we approach the Dewatto estuary, a resident heron flaps away. A dozen Canadian geese waddle across a mud bank, slip into shallow water and glide out to the bay.

Splash! Seconds later another splash sparkles the calm surface. Then the swell of the bay explodes into life and shimmies with action. Fish are everywhere. Coho break the water, leaping, side-flipping, exposing pale white bellies and slapping to break loose egg skeins in an overture to their dance of reproduction.

Moments later a loud motor boat barrels down the river pushing high walls of wake, disturbing everything in its path. Gulls rush skyward. A cormorant dives fast right in front of the oncoming danger and doesn't dare resurface till all is quiet.

An elderly couple harvest oysters from the low tide oyster beds. Three small boats bob up and down on the bay, filled with fishermen excited by the return of salmon.

We hike inland from the estuary to where the Dewatto becomes a shallow stream. I stare into pools milling with coho, chum and cutthroat trout. Then, attempting to stay as anonymous as possible, I edge closer to watch fish as they ruffle loose sand and gravel to prepare spawning beds. But the salmon, even though preoccupied, see me, swing around and race ten yards downstream. I wait unmoving and non-threatening till they return to their vital task. Most fish measure fifteen to twenty inches. A dozen or so battered and exhausted coho, black, with scraped reddish sides, top out at thirty inches. Groups of fish thrash compulsively, toss and roll through the water, while others hover in deep pools on the far side of the river.

Fish in the pools wait patiently till rain swells the river to ease their passage upstream to spawning grounds embedded in distant memories of conception. Do they consciously remember their route, or is their journey purely instinctual? I can't tell how many of these returning salmon are direct offspring of returning salmon who mated naturally or whether they are the result of the million eggs a year released in this stream to increase the population. Eggs deposited four years ago have produced record numbers of returning fish. Perhaps in four years an even larger percentage of salmon hatched from these eggs will return, another year closer to a natural cycle.

☼

A week, and three inches of rain, later, salmon have arrived at spawning grounds in the Tahuya River. Along our stretch of riverbank.

Squads of dark gray and pink coho leap, wriggle, and fling themselves over small rapids toward our land to spawn wherever an open patch of sandy riverbed offers a womb for their eggs. The fish, vivid pink and red, brightest in larger males, splash and zip up the swollen stream with the urgency of fire trucks heading to a blaze. After conquering the rapids, three or four dozen ten-to-twelve pounders cluster in front of the logjam, most of them treading water in a deep hole under the far bank.

A protective male guards a group of females while they slap bottom sand and gravel with strong tails to gouge troughs for egg laying. A shimmering, quivering female drops her eggs. The male aligns himself alongside and, with long orgasmic body shudders, spurts his milt onto the waiting eggs. The female then buries the fertilized eggs in her gritty sand redd on the river bottom and in five minutes the mating ritual is complete. Their life is almost over. And a new generation begins. I'm filled with awe to witness such an intimate scene.

Standing ankle deep in shallows of a side stream riffle, I'm quietly enthralled by the festival of procreation underway in the main channel. Suddenly, a jolt. A muscular ten-pound coho writhes and flips across my boot. A charge of concentrated salmon energy shivers through me. This fish has one goal on his upstream odyssey: to return to where he knows he must return. No obstacle of a yellow rubber boot can discourage this coho's focus and determination.

A single chum painstakingly digs a redd in a small private pool away from the other salmon, awaiting a chum mate. More than ninety percent of returning salmon in the Tahuya River are coho.

I watch the spawning rituals for hours, with deep gratitude for this magical place where I witness the source of future salmon generations. I hope to watch this same dance of mating, death and rebirth on this salmon stream for many years to come. Rain begins to fall, lightly at first, pitting the river with tiny circles, then heavier with widening rings that add to ruffled water patterns of the thrashing fish. I retreat up the hill and leave the coho to reproduce in peace, elated and honored to have witnessed this essential and amazing dance of renewal.

The next morning I run downhill to see if the salmon are still there. I half expect them to have disappeared overnight and that yesterday's creative celebration was a mirage. Loud splashes prove me wrong as I approach the stream. The fish are as dedicated as ever to the completion of their final purpose. Weak sun skims obliquely across the swollen river, turning it to a stream of gold where red-tinged coho spawn, spawn and spawn. Again I watch in awe.

☼

The Dewatto River has a far higher percentage of chum salmon than in the Tahuya and the run is earlier. A week after watching coho spawn on our stretch of river, I hike along the Dewatto to a small creek that runs into the main stream. Dozens of tattered chum summon last bursts of energy to muscle up the creek, their journey nearly over. Salmon swim feebly in final stages of life. I watch a chum draw faint breaths, the rise and fall of its tired body barely visible. Seconds later, glazed fish eyes stare lifeless.

Further up the creek the stink of rotting fish rises in a fog from creek banks. I gag from the stench. Bloated carcasses, mottled with pale yellow fungus, pile up three or four together against logs. Recently beached corpses gaze glass-eyed and grotesque. Receding lips on wide-open mouths bare razor sharp lower teeth. Older corpses leer with bird-pecked eyeballs and gaping dark eye sockets. Further upstream the stench is stronger

199

yet. Dead fish hang limp on snags in the river. Dozens of lifeless bodies fester on the banks.

This orgy of fish death would be ghoulish and horrific except for knowing the absolute rightness of the scene. Moldering fishes return to the eco-system as valuable food for hatching salmonids. Decomposing salmon flesh feeds plant life along the river, bugs feed on the plant life, salmonids eat the bugs and the cycle of life goes on. When I remember this, the decaying bodies are no scarier than piles of decaying leaves becoming mulch for spring growth. I hope that my own death will be of equal value.

CHAPTER 31

Laʌt Beʌt Honey

BEFORE DAWN we're on the road to bring last hives from Quilcene foothills to the lowlands for winter, hurrying to reach the yard before bees take off at sunrise for a morning flight. Misty cloud hovers around the boom truck all the way, so we need not be concerned. The bees won't be out in drizzle even though half-a-dozen scrawny flowers still bloom beside the road: wilted Shasta daisy, hardy thistle, tansy ragwort and a yellow penstemon.

At the bee yard, moisture beads saturate the air and only one or two brave or foolhardy bees bumble around outside the hives. I'm soon wet and cold, my sneakers and socks soaked through, and I regret not wearing heftier gear.

The bees are in a crummy mood in the stay-at-home weather. They have never liked us at this yard. They've had a rough year and do not want us around. Guards zap to surround us like squad cars at a bank heist. Quick to pull my veil over my head, I feel off-center and unprepared.

We take down the bear fence and stuff wire closures into the hive entrances. In a careless moment I push a mesh too far into a hive. When we lift the hive with the boom, a gap opens between the wire netting and the base that we forgot to staple to the bottom box. Duct tape to the rescue. Immediately. But not before dozens of bees pour through the crack to watch their home lurch and swing through the air.

Beekeeping demands constant awareness and attention as we work with heavy equipment and boxfuls of armed bees. We often make mistakes. I often space out in the intensity of bee buzz. Even with careful checking that every crack and hole is secured by the miracle of duct tape, there are always clever bees who escape to defend their hive. I cannot blame the bees when they are defensive. How would we feel if we were suddenly trapped inside our home, lifted off the earth, clunked down on a noisy vehicle and jostled off to who knows where? On top of having the larder raided not long before.

We drive out of the foothills with our full load of hives in thick mist that swirls through red, gold and orange woodlands. Then there's cautious fog-bound freeway driving while watching for reckless drivers unaware of the thousands of armed hazards hidden in boxes on our big white boom truck.

Roy has prepared a yard at the eagle nest viewpoint where we will over-winter these hives, a site with easy access and the promise of early spring blossom. Yesterday he cleared weeds and set up stands to keep boxes off the soggy winter ground.

By the time we arrive at the site we're tired and anxious to unload and go home. But we're in for a surprise. The one hive we left at the yard during the summer has been vandalized. Today. In the last few hours. And not by a bear. The hive, three boxes high, has been knocked down and the boxes scattered. A long tree branch, used to wreck the hive, lies on top of the overturned boxes. Distraught bees fill the air and crawl on the ground, buzzing and stumbling in extreme distress. Why would someone do this?

Did someone nearby watch Roy prepare the site yesterday, decide they didn't want bees in the vicinity and left us a message that our bees are not welcome? There are no homes within a hundred yards, this is privately owned land, and we have the owner's permission to keep the hives here. Perhaps the damage is the end result of a teenage dare?

We consider our options and reluctantly choose to take the bees to a safer location. We re-load the hive-stands that Roy set up yesterday, on top of our already full truck. I take photos of the vandalism to give to the local newspaper hoping that a sympathetic reporter will publish a story about the benefits of bees. Perhaps a story might deter future vandalism.

With no other site prepared, we take the hives to the nearby Beard's Cove yard, immediately improvising extra spaces at the far end of seventy hives already there. But we cannot drive the truck close to the newly created spaces to unload with the boom and must offload at the entrance to the yard.

Using a hand-truck, we wheel the heavy hives one by one over bumpy ground through the existing hive rows, then manually lift the boxes onto hive stands. Despite a cool drizzle, this is hot grueling work, especially since unexpected. Sweat pours down inside my bee veil and my glasses slip off my nose. Eventually, after far more work and time than anticipated, all the hives are safely in place for the coming winter months.

Despite today's vandalism, hives have sustained less damage than last year. We moved hives two weeks ahead of previous years, and this year all the bees are down from the mountains before hunting season.

For most of the winter, the bees will huddle inside their hives and cluster in a warm ball around their queen. They won't hibernate, but will move slowly and maintain a hive temperature around 92 degrees, rotating outer bees with inner bees so all have an equal chance of staying warm. On a rare sunny day in January they might fly out for a quick bathroom break, and in February brush wings through hazel catkin pollen. If they're hungry we've left ample honey in the hives for the months ahead. And to compensate for this wet and foggy climate we furnish extra insulation and moisture boards to keep the girls cozy in their winter quarters.

☼

By early afternoon I'm in my tee shirt and the temperature is warm enough to pull the last honey from one of the kitchen hives. To protect against the recent cold nights bees have glued a layer of propylis between the lid and the top box and it takes well-muscled prying to break open the cement-like insulation with a hive tool and enter the hive. Honey, capped and ready to go, plugs every cell in every frame in the top box.

After soaking a fume board with bee repellent and placing the board on top of the honey-filled box, I wait for disgusted bees to leave. Bees hate the putrid smell. I am not fond of it either. The stink works. Bees distance themselves from the foul frames with a mass evacuation to lower boxes. I take off the honey super, which weighs about forty pounds. Underneath, a deep box, three-quarters full of honey, will cover their winter needs.

Lifting each frame from the super, I gently brush away a crowd of reluctant bees who wander over the waxy surface. An orderly furry crowd files back into the hive entrance, not overly concerned by the recent robbery, or maybe they're not yet fully aware of the extent of the plunder.

I wheel the box of honey to the workshop for extracting later. This 'most local' liquid gold is precious, gathered from around our clearing. Our 'home' bees have pollinated the orchard, the vegetable garden and our flowerbeds and gathered nectar from nearby woodland wild flowers. And most important, they have visited the herb garden. I have watched them graze on a healing menu of thyme, oregano, chive, marjoram, sage, rosemary, lavender, echinacea, anise hyssop, valerian and rue, and that's just the cultivated herbs.

Often at farmers markets we hear that medical doctors have begun recommending that people eat local raw honey to alleviate allergies. This is something we've told people at markets all along. We appreciate that the information is now being shared with the general public.

I extract honey from the kitchen hive super. The reddish honey flows rich and thick with a complex herbal and slightly fruity taste, the exotic end product of nectar from many varieties of flower both cultivated and wild, not a simple single-blossom honey. This bucket of honey is for our own use through the winter months and for gifts for family and friends. I label these jars: Tahuya River Apiaries Special Edition.

CHAPTER 32

Neighbors No More

THE SOUND of revving engines and raised voices interrupts the forest silence as I unload our market booths and honey from the back of the Toyota. The neighbors must be leaving. They're pulling out either the travel trailer or the mobile home—hopefully both. What a relief! Perhaps the landowner has finally evicted them after their lease ended a week ago. About time. I'll check later.

The phone rings. I run inside and pick it up. Sharon is on the line.

"The police are here! The neighbors are being busted! Meth labs!"

Yes! Roy's email to our congressman paid off. We run up to the end of the neighbor's driveway.

Ten vehicles storm the property. Local law enforcement, the State Drug Division, HAZMAT and Animal Control surround the land and block exits. Lights flash, radios blare, officers shout. The scene is just like a TV crime show, except that this is the real thing, far more adrenaline pumping. We watch from a distance as deputies stomp through thigh deep salal around the front clearing.

"Over here, there's more stuff over here. Check this out."

Police uncover not one, not two, but three meth labs in the three shabby dwellings.

An officer yells to us, "Sorry it took so long!"

Another officer walks over. "We've known about these labs for a while but had to wait to get more evidence. We wanted to make as many arrests as possible, not just these people here."

Two women and a man sulk in the back of police cars. Animal Control drives away with the snarly pit bull. Where is the other man we have often seen here? We hope he's not lurking in the woods.

Searches uncover meth-manufacturing equipment in the mobile home, the motor home and the travel trailer, heroin on each of the suspects, six garbage bags full of mail stolen from five counties, and a 55-gallon drum of acetone. More criminal evidence shows up later.

Roy and I walk home elated. The heaviness of suspicion, paranoia and endless waiting for results begins to lift.

The relief echoes an unexplained feeling of lightness I felt during my early morning hike to the river, which must have held a premonition of our 'liberation'. But I would not have taken that morning hike if I'd known then about the impending police activity. If I'd taken my hike any later I would have again been startled by unknown men in the woods, this time by fully armed police officers creeping up hillsides to surround the neighbors.

Despite the sudden relief that our neighbors are gone, we don't know how much damage they did to their property. And in overflow, ours. Our main concern is whether chemical dumping has contaminated the water table. Tomorrow we hope to find out if, and how, the labs have affected the environment.

During the night, cold temperatures shift and warmer wind blows the first heavy rain of a winter storm across the peninsula. I listen to the welcome sound of rain on the roof. The prolonged dry spell of summer and fall has broken and in parallel time the long wait for resolution of our neighborhood problem draws to a close.

We hear good news. A preliminary environmental health report states that the neighbors ran a 'clean' meth operation. Minimal toxic traces were found in the three labs. The 'cookers' knew what they were doing. Police suspect that the meth was manufactured mostly in 'rolling labs' (plastic bins in the back of vehicles).

Toxic residue was found on the county road, a place I often sauntered past on my way to pick mushrooms, unaware that I skirted a chemical sewer. I remember feeling unwell a couple of times after crossing the entrance to their driveway, but had thought I was just hypersensitive and psychologically sickened by unfriendly vibrations.

The sewer line to the septic tank was never hooked up, so perhaps the water table is safe, but I wonder what four, and often more, people used as a toilet for six months. The sheriff's department hasn't examined the entire property. We suspect that other chemicals and toxins will be found buried in a small clearing behind the main clearing where we often heard suspicious digging. Perhaps that's where they buried their waste.

A Tacoma newspaper reports the police activity on our road. A man and two women were booked on suspicion of manufacturing meth, possession of heroin, mail theft, fraud and identity theft. The man had an outstanding warrant for first-degree escape. The chief suspect's boyfriend, who was not home at the time of the bust, also has a warrant out for his arrest. No wonder I was afraid to linger in the woods.

On a walk to Tall Trees Trail I look down the driveway to the neighbors' property. Deserted dwellings hunker dismal and wretched. The mildewed back door of the mobile home hangs open to the weather with a dirty bouquet of plastic flowers taped to the window. Piles of sodden trash litter the ground, soaked disintegrating leaves plaster dented vehicles and a desolate car sits with its trunk open to the weather. The hot tub fills with falling leaves and rain. No authorities have shown up yet to investigate the entire property.

The next day Sharon calls us at a quarter to eight on a dark drizzly evening. One of the women suspects has returned to the land with her boyfriend, the man who was gone from the land at the time of the bust. Why are they back? What are they here for? Hidden money? Buried drugs? Surely not the bouquet of plastic flowers. Sharon calls the sheriff.

Deputies arrive. The 'wanted' boyfriend dives into the trees. The deputies talk to the woman, but have no reason to hold her since she is out on bail, and the boyfriend, with whom she has a 'no contact order', has disappeared. She takes off in a truck she had hidden at the end of the road. The deputies decide not to search the forest for the boyfriend in the dark and also leave.

Roy and Ian bottle honey in the workshop. I lock the kitchen door. A wanted man is loose in the woods and might sneak into our clearing at any moment. What if he shows up on my doorstep with a gun?

Zap barks, but not continuously, so I am not overly concerned, although every childhood fear of the 'boogeyman in the woods' as well as every film, book and TV scenario of escapees grabbing hostages in isolated forest settings run through my mind. This really is a boogeyman in the woods. I have to trust that Zap would bark an uproar if a dangerously unfriendly person approached. But my guess is that the man probably just wants to find a way to connect with his girlfriend's vehicle.

☼

Today's newspaper reports that one of the arrested women has eight previous forgery convictions. The prosecutor requests a high bail, but the Judge sets the amount at only $10,000. The article states that raw sewage has been found all over the property, which answers my question about what the tenants used for a toilet. I wonder how toxic that sewage is after all the drugs they were taking. Needles were found scattered in the forest around Tall Trees Trail.

On a brief foray into trees adjacent to our property line Roy discovers several dug-over areas, a couple of discarded propane tanks and a bag of mail. He comes across a container of nasty looking liquid he describes as 'orange pus', and covered up holes less than seventy-five feet from our well. No 'officials' have shown up to further search the property since last week. The drama, like stubborn smog, refuses to lift from the neighborhood.

The Sheriff's department is writing a report for the environmental health department who will then decide how to act.

"Police know about the dug over holes and other evidence," the county chief narcotics detective tells Roy. "And it's almost certain the main woman suspect won't show up for arraignment later this week. We're overloaded. I know of a hundred meth labs in Mason County alone. It can take up to four years to gather enough hard evidence for arrests. You were lucky to wait only six months."

That night Zap barks intermittently all night, but we don't hear coyotes or any unusual sounds. We guess that the neighbors creep through the woods to quietly take whatever they can carry from the abandoned property. We will feel much safer once the chemically contaminated trailers have been destroyed and the land scoured.

Two days later, two of the three arrested neighbors plead not guilty to charges of meth manufacturing. The third, the woman with the eight previous forgery convictions and the $10,000 bail, fails to show up for her arraignment just as the detective predicted. Her 'wanted' boyfriend has not been found.

A week later, a hundred-mile-an-hour police chase late at night in neighboring Pierce County ends with the fleeing car, a white Mustang, going airborne, flipping several times and landing upside down. A man and a woman are admitted to hospital in critical condition. They might not survive. The driver is our 'wanted' ex-neighbor, and the passenger his girlfriend who failed to show up for her court date. The man is paralyzed from the neck down and the woman is in a coma, bleeding from her lungs, and her feet badly crushed.

Another meth related tragedy.

I have heard that remote forests in mountainous regions of Lao have been saved by war. A wasteland of land mines, no one will enter the Lao forests to cut the trees. Maybe the property next door will sit vacant for years while nature heals the wounded land. Maybe it will become a bird sanctuary. Maybe the human waste will become compost for fast new growth of plants and trees. Maybe a little too fast with all the meth. And maybe winter rain, like healing tears, will wash away fears that have haunted this forest community over the last seven months.

But healing for the humans involved could take a lifetime.

CHAPTER 33

APPROACH OF WINTER

RAIN FALLS. Hard rain. Drenching, soaking, splattering, bubble on puddle rain. Non-stop heavy rain for twenty-four hours. Rain like it will never end. But that does not keep me from responding to the lure of the river.

Hiking down the river trail I pause to honor the wet and dripping Guardian of the Forest. I offer thanks to the shaggy forest spirit for his ongoing protection of the river valley.

Falling water orchestrates a musical feast from every direction: raindrops ping and trickle from slick needled branches; staccato jazz riffs spatter my nylon rain hood; snare drum rhythms hiss against the evergreen canopy; waterfalls of moody tones drop from boughs to the woodland floor. In the background, the river is an entire string orchestra, swelling an ecstatic crescendo of racing water. The rain chorus and river symphony unite in an celebration of melodious wet.

The river has risen many inches since yesterday morning. I can no longer see through the dense water, but know that the salmon are long gone to smaller creeks and side streams. Rowdy water pushes and pulls at a plump dead fish caught on a branch midstream, its limp gray body bent double by the current.

I can no longer walk where I walked two days ago when water drifted in a lazy flow. Eddies rush and swirl past. Muddy water churns and wrestles new channels through the logjam while creamy foam spurts and pours over logs that one week ago protruded high above the surface.

The main beach has shrunk; other smaller beaches have completely disappeared. Drowning beach plants stretch out limbs like distress flags in shallow but rapidly rising water, while their bent stalks cling desperately to water-pummeled roots. Raindrops dance incessant rings on the river surface. The world has become liquid, an aquasphere ruled by Gods of falling water. The land needs gills to assimilate all this moisture.

Along the banks, soaked alder trunks slide rain rivulets onto tree-hugging moss anklets that look like dancers' rumpled leg-warmers, furry boots dripping moisture on a wet day. Drenched cities of pearly oyster mushrooms and fungus tumble from rotting bark; wet red maple arrows poke skyward from beaver chewed stumps; water dribbles down the beginnings of alder catkins that dangle over the river. I live in a water world, a kingdom of rain, a universe of wet.

The river valley welcomes its yearly transformation by water.

By the next day the beach has entirely disappeared. Water gushes down from clear-cut hillsides upstream where no deep root systems are left to sustain the heavy rain. Another three inches and the river will lunge outside its banks and flood the valley. Huge volumes of water, the color of lentil soup, pour through and over the logjam. I wonder how many thousands of tons flow through here each winter. More like millions.

Jutting at a precarious angle parallel to the tumultuous river is a massive stump where I often perch in summer above tranquil water and where in fall I sit for hours and watch salmon. A spindly young fir that took root at the crown now stretches almost horizontal to the river as water sucks at what is left of the naked stump root system, ready to tip the fir into the water. Upended decaying ten-foot roots protrude over the

213

current, only a matter of time and storm before the whole mass plunges downstream to crash into the logjam.

Exhilarated and emboldened by the surge and roar of the river and the steady downpour, I creep out along one of the slippery roots and climb onto the soaked mossy crown. The stump clings to the bank like a disintegrating loose tooth, unsteady, wobbling slightly as water rushes through and around the remaining, barely anchored, roots.

Water races under me, hissing, frothing, sparkling. Tumbling sticks, broken branches and trunks rush by impatiently, only to slam against the tangled obstruction of the logjam. Muddy foam-crested water flashes past. The whole stump jiggles and sways above the thundering bronco swollen river. I ride the electric edge of danger.

But I have known enough excitement this fall. Rather than be thrown and tossed as just another piece of flotsam into the logjam, I slide back down the wet roots of my treacherous perch to the riverbank.

From the safety of the shore I succumb to river hypnotism as the water rolls, roars, swirls and pours through the valley, leaping in mini-Niagaras through and over the logjam, biting greedily at underbanks and claw-like stumps. I surrender as a willing participant to the process of transformation by water.

☼

Stars blink and tremble in the vast silence of a clear predawn sky. Above the tree-line horizon of the clearing, the bright sliver of a crescent Moon hovers with Mars and another planet conjunct nearby. Lit by her two close companions, the Moon's entire luminescent globe glows faintly in the crisp night sky.

After a frosty dawn, rays of diluted sunshine flood the clearing with a pink-tinged misty glow, illuminating one of the kitchen hives to look like a Chinese pagoda. Inside the honeyed temple the bees hum quietly, snuggled sister-to-sister in a ball around their queen for coming wintry months. I rename the hive 'The Temple of the Bees'.

I hike the river trail. All deciduous leaves have fallen from their summer heights, leaving liberated alder and maple-choked woodlands to breathe freely all the way down through a disheveled anarchy of naked boughs to the damp earth. I stretch my arms wide and breathe my own freedom in the spaciousness of these crisp winter woods.

The faint smell of wood smoke drifts through the valley.

An eagle pipes a shrill reedy call. He perches with his back to me on a snag by the river, his white head scanning the eastern horizon. He hasn't seen me. I creep to the riverbank and squat before he knows I am there, determined to sit for a while in his presence. But I am too optimistic. He senses my furtive glance, swivels his neck, peers down with a beady imperious eye, gathers himself up like a diver before a high dive, effortlessly unfurls his wings, lifts off and nonchalantly flies away. Next time, I will keep my eyes to the ground and talk quietly, out loud, about what a wonderful view the eagle has, how magnificent he is, and how much is appreciated from a different perspective. Communication is all-important, with no sneaking around and furtive glances.

I wander along the frosty riverbank, from the corner of my eye watching for the return of the eagle to his perch. Downstream, lazy mists drift off sparkling water. The logjam, resting after the recent commotion of flood and chaos, takes on a special beauty, like old familiar furniture, scratched and imperfect but comforting with character and eccentricity. Glistening licorice ferns tumble from a mossy logjam-trunk. Upstream, shafts of weak sunlight flash and shimmy across the winter river. Blue water echoes blue sky.

Suddenly, with no warning, the earth gives way under my right yellow boot and my leg disappears to my thigh in an underworld hole where floods have washed earth from stump roots. My attention immediately shifts from the circling eagle overhead. Brought to ground level in a whimsical Alice in Wonderland world, in a moment of stillness after the fall, I know the magic of a different point of view. Moss speaks to me with sparkling drips of melting frost that roll from green fur tongues. Fungus, liverwort and lichen shine fresh and full of life. Shimmering lace webs hung with iridescent droplets wink at me from every twig and blade of winter grass.

Above, the eagle's silvery call.

POSTSCRIPT

LONG AFTER the neighbors left, a shadow of darkness continued to haunt the community.

Sharon and her grandchildren from the horse ranch opposite moved to another state, other neighbors divorced and the Tall Trees Trail forest fell victim to the saw. Escalating stress of that summer began the unraveling of my relationship with Roy. But for six wonder-filled years I was blessed to experience living 'in place' and to learn from the bees on the Olympic peninsula. I will always be grateful for that.

Even though I left North Mason County at the beginning of 2005, I often visit friends who live by the Tahuya River and wander in forests and around hidden lakes. The river still shimmies with sky reflections, salmon spawn and eagles return each winter. Nature has reclaimed the meth lab property.

As this book goes to press I hear news that the meth lab property has been sold and new owners have cut trees on the land and burn huge stump piles. Although I mourn the loss of any stand of large trees, perhaps the fire and smoke will cleanse the land of any lingering dark vibrations.

Roy still watches over hives in North Mason County, sells hive products at farmers markets and through his website at www.hiveharvest.com.

May honeybees fly to pollinate the earth and sweeten our lives for many years to come.